Finding Fonda

SEVENTY YEARS OF LOVE, LIFE, AND LAUGHTER

A ROMANTIC MEMOIR BY

RITCHEY MARBURY

Finding Fonda

SEVENTY YEARS OF LOVE, LIFE, AND LAUGHTER

A ROMANTIC MEMOIR BY

RITCHEY MARBURY

Copyrighted Material

Finding Fonda: Seventy Years of Love,
Life, and Laughter

Copyright © 2026 by Ritchey M. Marbury, III
RIMAR BOOKS
All rights reserved.

ISBNs: 979-8-9997533-3-5 (Hardback)
979-8-9997533-4-2 (Paperback)
979-8-9997533-5-9 (eBook)

Dedication

This book is dedicated to my wife, Fonda, who I love completely. We dated for seven years and have been married for 63 years and counting. That makes 70 years together and looking for many more. She lost her purse on a bus trip with our band and another boy found it. I took it from him so I could take it to her and meet her. Later we started dating and my family loved her so much that my grandmother told me to take her under the grape arbor and said, “We didn’t need to spend all our time picking grapes.”

Contents

CHAPTER ONE

Introduction

"Ritchey, you take your sweetheart under that grape arbor," said my grandmother. "And you don't have to spend all your time picking grapes!"

While in high school my family had a large grape arbor in the backyard. It was open on one side, but during grape season the other three sides and the top were covered with grapes and grapevines. My girlfriend, and sweetheart, was a drum majorette named Fonda Starnes. My grandmother loved her, and I believe she would have been happy if I married her immediately. I did eventually marry her, but that would be seven years later.

Fonda and I dated for seven years and have been married for 63 years. Now, for 70 years, Fonda and I have enjoyed a life of love, life and laughter together. This book is about those fun times. It tells how I found her and how we first met, our first kiss, and how I wrote love poems to her while we were high school sweethearts.

It also explains one of my most embarrassing moments on a date, when I took her into the men's bathroom, thinking it was the kitchen.

Fonda once told me she would not marry me even if I asked her. That was the same day I had planned a romantic proposal in one of the most romantic spots in all Tennessee. I did propose later and she accepted, but that was not a romantic proposal.

Our college years were up and down. Once, when I found Fonda was dating another boy while attending Tennessee Wesleyan College in Athens, Tennessee, I had my Georgia Tech roommate write Fonda a letter. The letter explained how my head was bashed open while playing intramural football. The idea was to make Fonda feel sorry enough to see me. It worked but not quite the way I wanted.

The book continues telling stories about fun adventures with our two children, our three grandchildren, and our great grandchildren. It tells how our daughter died of breast cancer, and how we mourned her death together.

After dating Fonda from 1954 until our wedding on June 16, 1962, and continuing to love each other for 63 years of marriage (and still counting), this is a book of mostly happy times. True, hard times came, and I talk about them in this book, but we never doubted our love for each other. This book concludes with a list of seven keys to a happy marriage based on our life experiences.

FONDA

RITCHEY

If you are looking for a book about mostly tragic happenings, this is not the book for you. If you want to read true experiences of love, life, and laughter, read on.

CHAPTER TWO

Finding Fonda

The Lost Purse

"Look, the new girl lost her purse."

The Albany, Georgia, high school band was just returning from performing at an out-of-town football game. We were all seated on a bus that stopped at the school to let everyone depart. One of the band members found a purse and explained that the new girl left it. To me that was the prettiest girl I had ever seen, and I quickly grabbed the purse from the boy holding it.

"I'll take it to her," I exclaimed. I had no idea where she lived, but I was going to find out. I rummaged through her purse, and sure enough, found her address.

She lived in an apartment building on Pine Avenue in Albany, Georgia, only about two miles from my home. The street was one of the main streets leading into downtown Albany. Her house was on the south side of the road. It was a small wooden house with a porch on the front.

I parked my car on the side of the road, walked up

the steps on the front porch, and knocked on the door. A nice-looking lady with a friendly smile answered the door.

"May I help you?" she asked.

"I'm looking for a girl named Fonda Starnes," I replied. "She lost her purse and I'm bringing it to her."

The lady answering the door was Fonda's mother.

"Fonda," I heard her call out. "There's a cute boy on the front porch that wants to see you."

I was delighted Fonda's mother thought I was cute. Maybe that would give me a good start in getting to know her.

Shortly Fonda came to the door. She had a big grin on her face and looked even prettier than when I first saw her.

"You lost your purse." I said. "I found it and I am bringing it back to you."

"Thank you," said Fonda. "Would you like to come in?"

That was exactly what I was hoping. I walked in and noticed a piano sitting in her living room.

"Do you play the piano?" I asked. "I see you have some sheet music sitting on your piano. It looks like the name of the music is *Deep Purple*. I can play that also. Why don't we sit down on the bench and play it together?"

We did. I am not a very good piano player, and Fonda is terrific, but I really enjoyed those few minutes with her. We chatted for a few minutes, and I found out she was going steady with another fella. Normally I am shy around girls, but she was too pretty for me to give up on so quickly.

I asked if I could see her again, and she said okay. Within another day or two I was back on her front porch knocking at the door. While inside, I saw a truck driving by with another fella sitting inside the truck blowing the horn. I quickly ran to the front porch and waved. It was her steady boyfriend, and my goal was to make him angry enough so that they would quit going steady.

It worked. Within a month or so I was the only one dating her. I'm sure many others tried, but I monopolized her time so much that no one else had a chance.

The Landlady

Fonda was a sophomore in high school at that time, and I was a junior. By the time she became a junior and I became a senior, we were dating on a regular basis.

Fonda had a sister named Carol Ann. They were both great girls, but with very different personalities. Fonda was shy and always had that innocent look about her. Carol Ann was a little more vivacious.

I remember one day Fonda stepped into some flowers in front of their apartment building. While Fonda and her sister were standing outside looking at the damage Fonda had caused, the landlady walked up.

"Carol Ann, why did you do this?"

"Carol Ann didn't do it," explained Fonda. "I did it."

"No, you didn't," stated their landlady. "You are too sweet. That Carol did it."

With that the landlady took the water hose and began squirting Carol Ann with water, soaking her completely, while Fonda watched innocently.

Fonda had then, and still has, that completely shy and innocent look about her. Everyone seeing her thinks she must be almost perfect, and I still think so.

The Date that Never Was

In about a year Fonda and her family moved to a brick duplex building on Fifth Avenue. I liked that because it was only a few blocks from where I lived on Maryland Drive. At the beginning of the school year, I would ride my bicycle to school and then ride her part way home after school on the back of my bicycle. Often, we would stop at the corner of Slappey Drive and Second Avenue and chat, sometimes for as long as an hour before leaving to go to our separate homes.

I was working for my father at the time doing land surveying. I love surveying and most of the time surveys were in wooded or vacant areas. We also had a project that involved surveying the sanitary sewer system within the city of Albany, Georgia. I was in charge of that survey.

One afternoon I found myself surveying the sanitary sewer line located directly in front of Fonda's home. There was a manhole directly across from her front door.

My job was to climb to the bottom of the manhole and measure its depth. In those days there were no safety measures required and the way we verified the manhole did not contain poisonous gases, was to look for roaches. If roaches were crawling around the bottom of the manhole, then it was safe to enter.

I saw the roaches and proceeded to climb to the bottom of the manhole. After determining the diameter of the sanitary sewer and measuring its depth, I climbed out. I don't think there were any roaches crawling over me when I climbed out, but I smelled like rotten eggs. I looked up, and there was Fonda, sitting on her front doorsteps.

"How about a date?" I asked.

Fonda didn't even smile. She just got up from her chair on the front porch, opened her front door, and walked inside. We did not go on a date that night.

We did go on a date the following week. Before our date, however, I made sure to shower, put on clean clothes, and stay out of sanitary sewer manholes.

Our First Kiss

I dated Fonda almost every Friday night. Her dad had a strict curfew. I was to have her home no later than eleven o'clock in the evening. If I got her home a few minutes early, we would stand on her front doorstep and chat. As soon as the time reached eleven, her dad would be inside and begin coughing with loud obvious coughs. I would then nervously leave, and Fonda would go inside giggling.

I wanted to kiss Fonda the first time I saw her but was too shy. Sometimes I would almost get up the nerve while standing on her front porch. Before I could kiss her, however, I would hear her dad coughing, and I just said goodbye and left.

Finally, one evening, I got her home about thirty minutes early. I had an idea. I took her to the side of her house where her dad could not see us from his front window. Lying on the ground was a small toy, a "Tootsie Toy Convertible."

"Look at that Tootsie Toy Convertible," I said.

"Where?"

As she looked down, I gave her a quick kiss. A quick kiss was all I had nerve enough to do. She didn't slap me. That was good. I kissed her again. She kissed me back. If I wasn't already in love with her, I fell completely in love with her at that moment. It would be almost seven years before I got the nerve to propose.

CHAPTER THREE

High School Years

Jacksonville Beach Band Trip

High school was a fun time. Fonda and I dated almost every Friday night. We played in the Albany high school band together, and we sat on the bus together when the band went on out-of-town trips to football games. Our first official date was on a band trip to Jacksonville Beach Florida. Our band was performing there, and we also had some free time to visit the beach.

Fonda and I strolled along the beach, hand in hand, and watched the rides and shows. One of the shows was a "ring the bell" demonstration. The show was promoted as a "test of strength." A visitor to the show would test their strength by swinging a mallet to send a weight up a vertical tower to ring a bell at the top.

Football players tried and failed. Bodybuilders tried and failed. Weightlifters tried and failed. Then one of the football players that I knew asked me to try. I didn't want

FONDA AS HIGH SCHOOL MAJORETTE

to embarrass myself, so I, at first, said no. They continued to tease and nag me until I finally agreed.

I don't know if the apparatus was rigged or if I actually was the best contestant, but I ran the bell three straight times. I won a teddy bear for Fonda and was the hero of the afternoon. Fonda and I sat together on the bus as we rode home that evening, her head on my shoulder.

My Most Embarrassing Moment

One evening Fonda and I were invited to go to dinner together at a local clubhouse. The host provided a wonderful meal which we all enjoyed. When the meal ended, Fonda and I walked out the door and then remembered we had failed to thank the hosts. The clubhouse was rather large with separate restrooms for men and women close to the kitchen. It was late and I was anxious to leave. I grabbed Fonda by the hand and pulled her into the nearest door.

"Wait, wait," came a voice from inside the door.

Fonda tried to get outside, but I continued to pull her inside.

"Wait," the voice said again. When I looked up, I realized what I had done. I had not pulled Fonda into the kitchen. I had pulled her into the men's restroom. We left quickly without going back to thank the host.

Love Poems to my Sweetheart

I didn't know what to do after that, so I decided to write her a poem. I called it "My Gal."

MY GAL

The earth and the sky and the birds in the trees
Send whispering echoes to me through the breeze.
They tell of blue eyes and of long flowing hair
That waves in the wind of the velvet night air.
They tell of a girl with a form so divine
Not Venice's beauty could be so sublime.

She walks down the beach, and she gathers some sand
That changes to diamonds inside of her hand.
She smiles at a bird as she strolls on her way
And starts it to singing the rest of the day.
She's quite a good sport with a Christian like love
She's just like an angel from Heaven above.

"Awake!" cries the earth. "Quick, look!" speaks the sky.
"Go get her!" the birds all exclaim with a sigh.
I awake from my mirth. I open each eye
And look at a beauty not Pharaoh could buy.
'Tis my gal; not a sham, not a lie.

I don't know if the poem impressed Fonda or not, but her

sister seemed to get a lot of laughs from it. Fonda told me her sister would grab a handful of sand and tell Fonda to change it to diamonds.

When I first gave the poem to Fonda, I spelled angel, A N G L E. I had tried so hard to impress her and the first time I wrote her a poem I misspelled one of the most important words. She quickly learned that I was a very bad speller. I still am.

That wasn't the only poem I wrote for Fonda. We both had an English teacher in high school by the name of Billy Bragg. He taught us the format for writing sonnets. I decided to write a sonnet for my girlfriend, Fonda. Here is that sonnet.

FONDA

To have a girl as lovely as the sun-
Light on a daffodil that blooms at dawn
Unfolding gracefully with care that none
Might say it lacks in worth or charm its own.

To know that she's as pure as winter snow,
As virtuous as the stars are high above,
As upright as the tallest oaks that grow,
As gentle as a lamb, there stands my love.

I love her for her smile, her faithfulness,
Her tears for me when I must bid farewell.

I love her for her prayers and cheerfulness
Which spur me onward, never let me fail.

Yes, she's an angel, rare as finest gold.
Sublime and fair, she's locked within my soul.

I did spell "angel" correctly that time.

I don't know if writing poems to my girlfriend was helpful or not, but I tried everything I knew how to do to impress her. It must have worked. She married me several years later.

Fonda Eats Rattlesnake

Not everything I did with Fonda was romantic. I had a good time teasing her and playing tricks on her. One time was when I took her on a dinner date to a friend's house. His name was Wade Whitley, and he lived on a large plot of land near the Flint River. He invited several couples over for dinner including Fonda and myself.

We decided to have a good time with our dates. We told them we had prepared a special dinner for them. The main dish would consist of the best meat on the market. We didn't tell them what the meat was, but we assured them it was a delicacy they would all enjoy.

Many of our high school friends were there with their dates. The meal was served on a wooden table with benches in the front yard of Wade's house. The table was decorated immaculately with a white clean tablecloth, paper plates, paper napkins, and disposable utensils. Wade and I brought the meal to the table and served each individual plate meticulously.

Everyone enjoyed the meal and most said it tasted like something between roast turkey and baked chicken. Our dates all enjoyed the meal. Then our dates wanted to know exactly what they had eaten. We gave them a certificate. The certificate stated, "Welcome to the Rattling Rattlers Association." Everyone had eaten a delicious serving of baked Timber Rattlesnake.

When I took Fonda home that night, she did not seem a bit surprised. She said, knowing me, I would probably do something like that. I believe she really felt a little nauseated knowing she had eaten rattlesnake, but she never let me know it.

A Kiss Beneath the Grape Arbor

Both of my grandmothers loved Fonda. My mother's mother especially loved her. After she met Fonda, she never wanted me to date anyone else and was ready for me to marry her immediately.

In my parent's backyard there was a large grape arbor. It was about twenty feet wide, twenty feet long, and about ten feet high. Woven wire fencing covered three of the sides and the top. Only one side was open. During grape season the grapes completely covered all three sides and the top.

My grandmother, my mother's mother, asked Fonda and me to sit down for a little talk. She was really a little matchmaker and sometimes reminded me of Granny in the TV show, Beverly Hillbillies. She was much smarter, but just as much a matchmaker.

"Ritchey," she said. "Do you and Fonda like grapes?"

"Sure we do."

"Good. Then Ritchey, you take your sweetheart over to your house and tell your parents you are going to the grape arbor to pick some grapes, and you don't have to spend all of your time picking grapes."

I may have been naïve, but I sure understood that message. I did take Fonda to the grape arbor, and we did not spend all of our time picking grapes. We shared a kiss beneath the grape arbor.

Fonda Plays Golf

Fonda was always popular, although she didn't know it. I kept her so busy that other boys didn't have an opportunity to spend time with her. She did, however, once indicate an interest in golf. Immediately, my friend, Wade, said he would teach her.

Of course, I was not completely happy about Fonda seeing any other boys, but I had no choice. Wade made up his mind he was going to teach her.

It was a sunny afternoon at a local driving range. The range had a separate location for each person driving the golf balls. Wade purchased a small bucket of golf balls and sat them beside the first vacant tee he could find. Fonda was ready.

Wade first showed Fonda the correct way to grip a golf club. Fonda thought it was awkward but tried hard to do it correctly. Wade stood behind Fonda, bringing his right arm around her right arm and his left arm around her left shoulder. After several tries, Fonda was ready to swing the golf club by herself.

Wade took one step back, but not quite far enough. Before he could react, Fonda swung the club. She hit something, but not the golf ball. What she hit was Wade's head. It didn't knock Wade down, but it did give him a strong headache. That was the last time Wade ever gave golf lessons to Fonda, or to anyone else to my knowledge. I must admit I thought it served him right for spending time with my girl.

Fonda Breaks Our Date

Fonda was so popular (although she still didn't know it) that many boys wanted to date her. Finally, the most popular boy in school decided to ask her out. It was on the same day that Fonda had agreed to go to a movie with me. Fonda accepted the boy's invitation and gave me some excuse as to why she could not go with me.

I wanted to see the movie, and did not want to see it alone, so I invited another girl to go with me. We had no romantic interest in each other but were friends. I think she even knew I had first asked Fonda to go with me

My date and I walked down the middle row and found seats near the front of the theater. Another couple sat directly in front of us. It was Fonda and her date. I made sure Fonda saw me. I was hurt and upset. My date thought it was funny. I said I would never date Fonda again. I did not date girls that broke dates. I went for several weeks without asking Fonda for a date.

Fonda and I Get Back Together

I had decided I would never ask Fonda for a date again. Our time together was over! What a dumb decision. I still loved her. It seemed our friends understood that.

One day Fonda and I both received a letter. It was an invitation to a class party. My invitation said Fonda was to be my date. Her invitation said I was to be her date.

"OK, I'll take her," I said sarcastically. "The invitation said she was to be my date, and I don't break dates."

It is a wonder that Fonda even agreed to go the way I acted, but she did. We had a marvelous time. I was too shy and too proud to admit I still loved her, but we did begin seeing each other again.

The Party that Never Was

Fonda and I continued to date every week. Soon Fonda and one of her good friends decided to play a trick on another classmate. They prepared dinner invitations to a party at another friend's house. They picked dates for everyone and mailed the invitations. There was only one catch. The host did not know about the party.

As soon as the named host family discovered the invitations, they were furious. They soon discovered that Fonda and her friend were the culprits. Immediately they demanded Fonda and her friend send letters explaining what they had done and retract the invitations. Reluctantly they did so, but that was not the end.

I decided I would have some fun. I asked a neighbor if he would help with my plan. Soon the plan was in effect. The neighbor telephoned Fonda.

"Hello. Is this Miss Starnes? Miss Fonda Starnes? This is special agent from security investigating a group of false invitations sent through the mail. Are you the guilty party?"

I don't know what Fonda's answer was, but I know she was frightened. As fate would have it, the next day an announcement came over the school speakers.

"Would the following individuals please come to the principal's office?" My name was among those called.

Fonda really thought she was in trouble then. As it turned out, it was a holiday job offer for several of us that had worked for Kress Department Store in the past. The store needed extra workers for the holiday season and wanted to know if we were interested. I had worked there as a stock boy the past holiday season. (On a side note, Kress Department Store later became K Mart Department Store.)

I couldn't help myself. I told Fonda the principal wanted to know if I had any information about who used the U. S. Postal Service to send out false dinner invitations. After enjoying Fonda's reaction, I confessed to everything, including that I was the one who requested a neighbor to pretend he was a special agent from security. Fonda was relieved, mad, and tickled all at the same time.

The White Orchid and the Dress

Fonda and I continued to date all through high school, and we often went to school dances. I would ask Fonda before the dance what color dress she was going to wear. Then I would buy her a white orchid and give it to her to wear to the dance.

Fonda loved the orchid, and I was very proud of myself for remembering to give her the flower. After several dances Fonda wondered why I aways asked the color of her dress. I said I had no idea. My mother always just told me to ask what color dress you were wearing. Then I would just buy you a white orchid.

I later learned why I needed to ask for her dress color. I needed to get a flower that matched the color of her dress. I did not know that and always just bought her a white orchid. Lucky for me, a white orchid matched any dress color she would wear, so I did OK.

High School Graduation

I graduated from Albany High School in 1956. Fonda graduated in 1957. We continued to date and were still in love.

We each purchased a high school annual for the year 1956 and wrote a note to each other in the annual. The annual was entitled Thronateeska, which is a word meaning "flint picking up place" and refers to an area around Albany, Georgia, and the Flint River. It was the name of a Creek Village that existed on the banks of the Flint River centuries ago.

Fonda signed my annual on May 9, 1956, and wrote the following message:

Dearest Ritchey,

I've waited all year for this (you know, I thought I'd write a beautiful speech), but now that the time has come the words didn't. I could write a book on how wonderful I think you are, but words just can't express how much you've meant to me. I'm almost afraid to write (scared it might come true!) No, I was just joking.

I never regret a minute of it. You've been a wonderful friend and no girl could possibly wish for a better fellow! You're one of the finest Christian persons I've ever had the pleasure of knowing. I know that you'll always take God as your partner.

Don't forget our good times. I want (how could I?) After all, this has been quite a year, hasn't it? The good and the bad–I wouldn't swap it for anything in the world. Just think–if I hadn't lost my pocketbook it might never have happened. (What a shame!!!).

I never forget the times you tried to drown me, kidnap me, etc. Boy, it's been an unusual year!!! I really hate to see it end. I don't know what we poor little things will do without you big brave seniors!!! I know you'll have a ball at Tech.

Always stay just like you are now and maybe someday you'll have a "lovely wife and three sons." If you're real (that's for BB) good, you may even have four or five (imagine that).

Well, I'd probably be sitting here all night if I don't stop–so, just maybe I'd better not take a chance on it. Be good and don't forget me. (Philippians 4:13)

I love you,
"Fon"

I also wrote the following message in Fonda's annual:

Dear Fon,

My heart was cut to the very depths when I discovered that (Gasp!) Charlie was dead! I never thought one so high I could drop so low.

Remember the swell times we've had together. Eney, meney, miney, mo. Don't forget them, no no no! Remember our song, "September Song," and the trouble you have had with the strap on your band hat. May God bless you and go with you through every phase of life. Call me if I can ever help you in any way. God bless you again.

"88,"
Ritchey M. Marbury, III

At the time I wrote those comments, "Charlie's dead," was a way of saying that Fonda's slip was showing beneath her skirt. Also, the number "88," meant "love and kisses." As is obvious, I was still very naïve, and bashful, and was stupid enough to sign as though I were signing a bank check rather than signing a note to the girl I loved.

Fonda graduated from Albany High School in 1957. I wrote the following message in her annual that year:

Dear Fon,

You are one of the sweetest gals I know. I don't know when I've ever met a nicer or sweeter girl, or one with a nicer personality. I mean it. How you put up with me at times is more than I'll ever understand.

Remember the great times we've had together. The skating, the swimming, carpet golf, the movies, and even watching the rat at the zoo. I'll always remember them.

Best of everything at college and may God aid you in everything that you do. Stay like you are and I'm sure you'll have no trouble in life. When you find what you want, go after it and work towards it. You can go to the top in piano and most everything if you're willing to try.

God bless you and be with you always. He couldn't bless a cuter or nicer girl. Be good and don't forget me.

Love,
Ritchey, III

I was a little bolder when I signed Fonda's annual that year and signed it with the word "Love." That was a big thing for me. Many people just use the word, love, meaning they care about the person. When I used that word it meant I was "in love" with my sweetheart, Fonda Starnes. Five years later she would become my bride and wife, Fonda Starnes Marbury.

CHAPTER FOUR

College Years

Off to College

After graduating from Albany high school in 1956, I left home for Atlanta, Georgia, to pursue a degree from Georgia Tech in civil engineering. The following year, 1957, Fonda entered Valdosta State College. We continued to date when we came home from college on weekends and during the summers.

We wrote to each other often and continued to be much in love. Fonda even sent me a picture of her standing on a desk with my picture beside her. Every time I looked at the picture, I thought she was the most beautiful girl in the entire universe.

After about a year at Valdosta State College, Fonda's parents were no longer able to afford sending Fonda to college, and she moved to Atlanta, Georgia, to take a job there. I loved it. She was closer to me, and I could see her on a regular basis.

FONDA STANDING ON TABLE
NEXT TO MY PICTURE

FONDA AND RITCHEY FIJI ISLAND PARTY

During my sophomore year at Georgia Tech, I joined the fraternity of Phi Gamma Delta. It had the nickname, Fiji. Each year the fraternity had a social called the "Fiji Island Party." Since Fonda was living in Atlanta, I was able to invite her to go with me to the party that year. Everyone dressed up as Fiji Islanders. We had our picture taken at the party together.

We continued to date and go to various fraternity parties. We also had our picture taken when we later attended a more formal party.

Shortly after moving to Atlanta, Fonda's parents moved to Athens, Tennessee, and were able to send her to a nearby college, Tennessee Wesleyan College. Fonda had also moved to Tennessee with them.

I did not really like that. She was now about 160 miles away and almost three hours away. She and her parents shortly moved to Cleveland, Tennessee, which was about 120 miles away and a two hour drive. Still too far away.

FONDA AND RITCHEY AT FRATERNITY FORMAL

Ritchey Starts Graduate School

I graduated from Georgia Tech with a bachelor's degree in civil engineering in 1960. I then proceeded to apply to attend graduate school for a Master of City Planning degree from Georgia Tech. Due to one bad quarter at Georgia Tech, the head of the city planning department felt my grades were not good enough to allow me to be accepted. I requested an interview with the head of the department.

As I persisted in my request, the department head thought he found one way to get me to quit asking.

"We will let you enroll if you take the undergraduate courses we specify. You will take these five courses, and if you make an A in at least four of the courses and no less than a B in the other course, we allow you to enroll as a student on probation."

The courses included statistics plus four other courses. I accepted. I made an A in every course and was allowed to enroll as a student on probation. Over time I became friends with the professors, and they enjoyed having fun with me while telling others that I was the only student ever to be put on probation for making an A in every course. I eventually graduated number two in my class.

The Cut on my Head

Fonda and I both dated other people while at college, but we both were still really in love with each other. Fonda seemed interested in some boy there at Tennessee Wesleyan and I got worried she may like him too much. The boy will go unnamed.

While in graduate school, many of us would play touch football after classes. One of those afternoons, I was playing quarterback when an opposing lineman banged his head on my forehead. I thought I had a hard head, but it was not hard enough. The blow left a large cut such that it bled profusely. It took several stitches to repair the damage.

Not wanting to miss any opportunity to gain sympathy from Fonda, especially when she might have another boyfriend, I thought of a plan. I had my college roommate, a student named Tom Guffin, write her a letter. I dictated the letter myself, but Fonda would believe it came from my roommate.

The letter told how I was injured in a football game and had a one-inch gash on my forehead. The bleeding was so intense that I had to go to the hospital for stitches. It said how I kept telling him how much I wanted to see Fonda but was afraid she was seeing someone else and would not see me. Everything in the letter was true, but a little embellished to gain Fonda's sympathy. It worked.

A short time later I drove to Tennessee Wesleyan College to see Fonda. The cut was mostly healed, and I only had a small bandage on my forehead. Fonda did see me, but made fun of the small bandage. She just laughed and said she was expecting to see my head wrapped in a large tourniquet. Maybe I should have done that. It might have been more effective. Still, I was able to spend time with her, and that was the goal.

The Proposal that Wasn't

Although I wanted to have my master's degree and a good job before marrying, I just couldn't wait any longer. I was ready to propose. I wanted this to be the most romantic and best proposal ever. One that Fonda would remember all her life.

Fonda would graduate this June, 1962. Maybe we could marry a week or two later. She always wanted to be a June bride, and I would make her one.

I studied to find what I thought was the most romantic place to propose. I found it. Lookout Mountain, Tennessee. From the top of the mountain you could see seven states. There was no more romantic place in all the South.

I would drive her there, show her how beautiful the scenery was, and then tell her how she was better and more beautiful than anything else around. I would then ask her to marry me.

When she said yes, I would put my arm around her, kiss her, and again tell her how much I loved her and that I would love her forever.

We were now at the top of Lookout Mountain. The view was beautiful. I could not have picked a better spot.

I went over what I would say in my mind to be sure I said it exactly right. I was ready to propose.

Then, before I could utter a word, Fonda spoke.

"Even if you asked me to marry you, I would say no."

I was crushed. I didn't know what I had done wrong. I thought I had done everything right. Without saying another word, I drove her home.

The Proposal

I loved Fonda too much to give up on her, and I really felt (or hoped) that she loved me. I was determined to propose, but this time it would not be a romantic one.

A few weeks after the "proposal that wasn't" we were driving from her home in Cleveland, Tennessee, to my home in Albany, Georgia. I felt scared of the same response but was determined to propose.

Halfway between Cleveland and Albany I found a secluded spot on the side of the road. I stopped.

"Will you marry me?" I asked.

"Maybe," Fonda replied.

"I don't want a maybe, I want a yes."

Fonda smiled. "Yes."

Then she kissed me.

We continued to Albany. I was the happiest man alive. I was going to marry my childhood sweetheart and the only woman I had ever truly loved. I then told her I did not yet have her an engagement ring. I wanted to be sure she would say yes before buying her one. That would come later.

When I told my family about our engagement, they were thrilled. I don't know who loved Fonda more, me or my family.

I wanted to buy Fonda an engagement ring with a flawless diamond because I thought she was the most flawless person I had ever known. My mother helped me find one from the best jeweler in town. I bought her a 110 carrot flawless diamond engagement ring. My family helped me pay for it.

Now it was time to give Fonda the ring. I was so proud of myself. I drove to her home in Tennessee to give her the ring, but I wanted to do it in an unusual way.

I told Fonda to wait in her living room while I went to another room. There I turned off all the lights except one light on a lamp. I had that light focused on her ring.

I went back into the living room, gave Fonda a pair of strange-looking sunglasses, and told her to put them on. I then escorted her into the room where her engagement ring was sitting beneath the lighted lamp. She laughed, put on the ring, and gave me a kiss. Our engagement was now official. We were both excited.

CHAPTER FIVE

Our First Years Together

Wedding Plans

Time to set a date and prepare for the wedding. Fonda was to graduate from Tennessee Wesleyan College in June 1962, with a degree in music. We planned the wedding for a couple of weeks later, June 16, 1962. Fonda would be a June bride.

On March 20, 1962, three months before our wedding, Fonda gave a piano recital at her college. She was magnificent and she was giving her own piano recital. The program is shown on the next page. She was nervous but gave an outstanding performance.

When she graduated, Fonda was not only president of her sorority, Kappa Delta but also president of the Delta Rho Mu Music Fraternity (the Laura T. Sherman Music Fraternity).

The Sunday, March 4, 1962, issue of the Albany Herald announced our engagement featuring a picture of Fonda.

TENNESSEE WESLEYAN COLLEGE

ATHENS, TENNESSEE

SENIOR RECITAL

Fonda Starnes, Pianist

Townsend Auditorium
March 20, 1962
8:00 p.m.

PROGRAM

Toccata in G-major ---------------------------- J. S. Bach (1685-1750)
Allegro Vivace
Adagio
Fugue

Sonata Op. 2, No. 1 ------------------------ L. van Beethoven (1770-1827)
Allegro
Adagio
Menuetto
Prestissimo

INTERMISSION (TEN MINUTES)

Moments Musicaux ---------------------------- F. Schubert (1797-1828)
Op. 94, No. 2
Op. 94, No. 3
Op. 94, No. 5

Prole Do Bebe (The Baby's Family) ---------- H. Villa-Lobos (1881-)
Branquinha (The Porcelain Doll)
Moreninha (The Paper Doll)
O Polichinelo (Punch)

Delta Rho Mu invites guests at the recital to an informal coffee honoring Miss Starnes in the Student Lounge immediately following the program.

FONDA'S PIANO RECITAL PROGRAM

A few days later, on March 9, 1962, the Albany Herald wrote an article in the Georgia Life column with the title, "Finds Honesty is Best Policy." It told how I found Fonda's lost pocketbook on an out-of-town bus trip to a football game.

The Tuesday, March 20, 1962, issue of the Atlanta Journal also featured an article about our proposed wedding with a picture of Fonda. Fonda was so beautiful that all the newspapers wanted to print her picture.

Wedding plans began in earnest. Fonda needed a wedding dress. We borrowed one from my cousin, Camille. I needed to select a best man. I chose my dad. Fonda needed a matron of honor. She chose her sister Carol Ann Creech.

We needed to select where to be married. We chose the First Methodist Church in Albany, Georgia. We needed to select who would perform the marriage ceremony. We chose J. Frederick Wilson, current pastor at First Methodist Church.

Fonda was honored with a shower on Saturday, April 14, 1962, given at the home of Mrs. William A. Ford. Fonda wore a beautiful pink embroidered taffeta, a princess-line dress and was presented with a white orchid corsage by the hostess. Special guests were my grandparents, Mrs. R. M. Marbury, Sr. and Mrs. Ida Van Houten. Fonda had a wonderful time.

We also needed to select a date. We chose Saturday, June 16, 1962, at 4 o'clock with a reception to be held right after the wedding in the Haley Memorial Youth Center, located in another part of the church.

Our Wedding

The big day! Fonda and I are getting married! I got up late since the wedding was to be in the afternoon. Many say they are nervous just before the wedding, but not me. I was excited. I had waited seven years to marry the girl of my dreams, and now it was happening.

I thought about how my car would be painted over with "just married" remarks, and my dad and I had an idea. I would hide my car, and we would ride to the wedding in dad's car. We would make it look as if Fonda and I were going on our honeymoon in my dad's car. We did just that.

The wedding went perfectly. Church decorations featured a myriad of candles. Giant white chrysanthemums were used on the altar and wedding urns held arrangements of white flowers. The background featured seven-branch candelabras with palms. Other candles were held by three-branch candelabras and candle trees. Pews were marked with white satin bows. Fonda wanted a lot of candles at her wedding, and she got them.

Carol Ann Creech, Fonda's sister, was her matron of honor. Her bridesmaids were Sue Ella Hankins, Joan Ellington, and Eva Lou Groves, who all went to college with Fonda. Suzanne Barela, Richey's cousin, who later married Waddell Hagans, was also a bridesmaid.

Of course there was a flower girl. It was Debra Lynn

Pictured left to right are Sue Ella Hankins, Joan Ellington, Fonda Starnes (Marbury), Carol Ann Creech, Suzanne Borella (Hagins), Eva Lou Groves, and at the bottom is the flower girl Debra Lynn Creech

Creech, Fonda's niece. Rusty Van Houten, Ritchey's cousin, was the ringbearer.

My dad served as best man. The groomsmen were Bradley Horton Baker, William Woolard Wingfield Jr., David Kammer, Charlie Sellers, Robert Arthur Soper, and William Henry Bunton Jr.

Mrs. Wallace Crouch played the organ with selections including "Venetian Love Song," "O Perfect Love," and traditional wedding marches. Mrs. Joseph Hugh O'Rouke, our next-door neighbor who had a beautiful soprano voice, sang "Through the Years," "I Love Thee" and "the Lord's Prayer."

FONDA AND I WALK DOWN THE AISLE TOGETHER AS HUSBAND AND WIFE

WEDDING PICTURE WITH FONDA'S PARENTS ON THE LEFT, FONDA AND I IN THE MIDDLE, AND MY PARENTS ON THE RIGHT

The pastor, Dr. J. Federick Wilson gave a few remarks and then asked, "Who gives this woman to be married to this man?"

Fonda's father replied, "Her mother and I do."

Fonda and I exchanged rings. Rev. Wilson continued, "I now pronounce you husband and wife. You may kiss the bride."

I gave my new bride a prolonged kiss (the audience laughed) and we walked down the aisle as husband and wife.

Immediately after the wedding the photographer took a picture of us with our parents. That picture is shown above with Fonda's parents on the left, my parents on the right, and Fonda and I in the middle.

FONDA AND RITCHEY

WEDDING CAKE

Our Reception

Immediately following the wedding, we had a reception in another part of the church building, the Haley Memorial Youth Center.

Then the fun began. First, we went outside to find my dad's car painted with "Just Married" all over it. Our plan worked. Mother and dad had a good time driving all over town in the "Just Married" car. The guests thought we were going on our honeymoon in my dad's car and painted it instead of ours.

When I drove up in our car, Fonda had forgotten something and had to go back into the church to get it. That gave the guests time to paint our car with "Just

DAD AND HIS CAR PAINTED “JUST MARRIED”

FONDA AND RITCHEY LEAVING FOR THEIR HONEYMOON

RITCHEY AND FONDA'S ACTUAL CAR WITH "JUST MARRIED" PAINTED ON CAR

Married" signs. Sometimes I think Fonda planned it that way so that our car would be painted. She really enjoyed all the signs on our car.

That was not all. As we were leaving to go on our honeymoon, Cindy Aspinwall, Ritchey's preschool cousin, jumped into our car and would not get out. After trying several times to get her out, we decided to ride around town and then take her back, hoping she would then get out. She didn't.

Her parents finally took her out of our car, and we were off to the Cloister at Sea Island, Georgia, where we would spend our honeymoon.

Our Honeymoon

Off we went, two people, just married, and very much in love. Our destination, Sea Island, Georgia, 185 miles and three- and one-half hours away. It was late. We were tired and we were hungry. We stopped in Waycross, Georgia, to have our first meal as a married couple at the Green Frog Restaurant.

SIGN AT GREEN FROG RESTAURANT

We spent our first night in a local motel there in Waycross. The next day we were off to the Okefenokee Swamp Park. I like to tell people that we spent our honeymoon at the Okefenokee Swamp Park. Actually, we only spent a few hours there and then were off to the Cloister at Sea Island, Georgia, our honeymoon destination.

At that time the road to Sea Island was a small two-lane asphalt road. Green grass and palm trees on both sides of the road created a vista of beauty few could match. When we arrived at the Cloister the view was even more picturesque. Palm trees, red, white and yellow flowers, and decorative signs told us we had arrived.

We were treated like royalty. For dinner, coat and tie were required. A small orchestra entertained us with violin, piano, and saxophone musicians. A "Do Not Disturb"

RITCHEY AND FONDA ON BICYCLE
BUILT FOR TWO

sign was posted outside our bedroom door. Breakfast was served the next morning in our room.

Fonda insisted on keeping everything neat and even ironed our clothes before allowing us to leave the room. When we went outside, we rented a bicycle built for two and pedaled around the island. Although there were pedals where both could pedal, I did most of the pedaling.

We went to the beach that afternoon. Sea Island is located on the Atlantic Ocean, and we enjoyed playing in the ocean waves. Then back to riding along the island on our bicycle built for two.

Later we visited Jekyll Island and the Jekyll Island Museum. Then on to St. Simmons Island to visit Fort Frederica. Fort Frederica was established by James Oglethorpe in 1736 to protect the southern border of Georgia from Spanish raids.

After only a few days, we returned home. We rented an apartment at Georgia Tech where I continued work on my master's thesis.

Apartment Living

Techwood Apartments, the apartment complex at Georgia Tech where Fonda and I made our first home, was tiny. To call it an "efficiency apartment" is an understatement. The apartment had one room that served as both a living room and bedroom. It did have a small kitchen and a small bathroom.

A couch in the living room served as our bed. When unfolded into a bed, it took up the entire room space and there was almost no room to walk around. It did have a small bookcase. We lived on the first floor.

Although Fonda eventually became a wonderful cook, that wasn't her talent when we first married. One day she was boiling water when I heard a scream. I rushed into the kitchen to find boiling water on fire.

Fonda cried, "Put it out. Put it out."

What did I do? I grabbed my camera and started taking pictures.

Fonda did manage to put out the fire, and I did manage to get some pictures. I enjoyed telling my friends that my wife was the only person I knew that could start a fire by boiling water.

I remember David Kammer, a former college roommate and good friend, came to see us one evening and

TECHWOOD APARTMENTS, OUR FIRST HOME

was not sure what apartment we lived in. He just stood outside the apartment parking lot and yelled, “Fonda! Ritchey!” until we heard him and let him in. We had already pulled out the bed from the couch and that took up the entire room. We had to fold the bed back into the couch to have room for David to visit us.

We had subleased the apartment from a couple that was away for a short time. With almost no notice, they returned and told us we had to move. We quickly found another apartment and moved in. The apartment complex, the Darlington Apartments, was only a few miles from Georgia Tech. We stayed there until time for me to enter the military.

CHAPTER SIX

Off to the Military

Basic Training

My master's thesis, *A System of Open Spaces for Outdoor Recreation in Metropolitan Areas*, was approved by two of the three required approvals. The head of the department, however, said I needed a little more research before approving.

I had taken four years of ROTC at Georgia Tech so that I could enter the military as an officer. I was required to serve two years after that. I had already received two years of extensions to work on my master's thesis, and the military would grant me no more.

My first three months in the military were to be at Ft. Belvoir, Virginia. The military said they did not want wives to go with husbands, but Fonda wanted to go, and I surely did not want to go without her. After all, we had only been married six months.

So, the first part of January, 1963, we packed all our possessions into our car and headed to Ft. Belvoir. The car was a small Plymouth Valliant, the same car we took on our honeymoon. We purchased a top car carrier to place some of our belongings that would not fit into the back seat or trunk of our car.

We rented a small apartment (not as small as Techwood Apartments) about a mile from the base. Fonda kept house and I went each morning from there to basic training.

It was tough. We were taught there were only three answers to questions, "Yes Sir. No Sir, and No Excuse Sir." We learned to crawl on our bellies while machine gun fire using live bullets blazed above us and only three or four feet above the ground. We built a Bailey Bridge across a small river in two below zero weather. We learned the importance of and how to use gas masks by being put into a room filled with chlorine gas and allowed to put on the gas mask only after standing in the room a short while without wearing the mask.

Inspections came early every morning. Fonda helped by spit shining my boots most mornings. A spit shine was where you spit on the top of the boot and then polished it such that the toe had a brilliant shine.

Once my name tag came loose and there was not time to sew it back on. Fonda took some bubble gum and pasted the name tag back on just before I left for inspection. The inspection went well until the inspecting officer noticed the loose name tag. Ripping it off he asked, "What is this lieutenant, chewing gum?"

"No sir," I responded. "Bubble gum."

The inspection did not go well for me that day.

I became sick during basic training with a temperature of 103 degrees. Fonda wanted me to stay home, but I knew if I did, I would have to start basic training all over again. I went to training early that morning, even with a 103-degree temperature. As luck would have it, there was a medical checkup that day for all trainees.

They stuck a thermometer in my mouth and sent me through the line to be checked. As I approached the counter, I looked at the thermometer. It read 104 degrees. I quickly shook it down to where it read 98.6 degrees. I passed the medical inspection.

I could hardly do the exercises and calisthenics. I was too sick, but I was not going to let anyone know. Fonda wanted me to go to sickbay, but I knew if I went, I would have to start basic training over again. I was determined not to do that.

Some way I managed to do the training requirements, but not well. I could hardly run. I could hardly do any pullups and only 10 or 15 pushups. I failed all the physical fitness requirements. After a week or two of training, the drill instructor recommended I be put back into the beginning class again. He sent me to the company commander for his approval. Lucky for me, by that time I had recovered.

The company commander put me through a series of physical fitness tests and marching exercises. I was proficient in everything, easily doing 50 pushups, 14 pullups in about 10 seconds, and precision marching. When the company commander asked what was going on, I stated that the drill instructor must have confused me with some other person. I was allowed to continue training.

No one could have a better wife during those days of mental and physical harassment. The stress was intentional to prepare us for the rigors of combat, but it was hard. During those days, Fonda would fix meals for me, mend and press my uniform, and even "spit shine" my boots. She never complained about my leaving early and coming home late. She just hugged and kissed me and continued to tell me how much she loved me.

After three months of training, I graduated. My assignment would be with the 538th Construction Engineer Battalion at Ft. Knox, Kentucky.

Arrival at Ft. Knox, Kentucky

As we drove into Ft. Knox, Fonda noticed the soldiers all saluting the car as we drove by. We still had our Plymouth Valliant with all our personal belongings in that one car. I told Fonda they were all saluting us because they saw her in our car and wanted to salute the prettiest girl they had ever seen. In fact, the car had a sticker on the bumper that indicated I was an officer. Enlisted personnel always saluted officers, even if they were driving by in an automobile.

We made our home at 5650 B Demoret Avenue. It was a two-story brick apartment building that housed lieutenant grade officers.

Later Fonda went into town to shop. On returning she saw flashing lights behind her. She paid no attention. She drove further. The car behind her continued to flash their lights. It was the military police. Fonda continued to drive on.

Finally, Fonda stopped. The military police pulled over and walked over to Fonda's car.

"Did you realize you were speeding?" asked the police.

"No," said Fonda. "I just stopped to tell you that there must be something wrong with your lights. They keep going on and off, on and off."

"Lady," replied the police. "You were speeding."

"No," said Fonda. "I wasn't doing anything wrong, but you had better get your lights fixed. They keep going on and off. They keep going on and off."

"Lady."

"You really had better get your lights fixed. They keep going on and off, on and off."

"OK lady," said the frustrated military policeman. "You just go on."

Fonda continued home. The military policeman just stayed there, scratched his head and must have thought about how he would explain that incident in his daily report.

Fonda always had that sweet and innocent look about her. Maybe that is part of why I love her so much. One look at her and a Bengal tiger would turn into a Ragdoll pussycat.

Our First Child is Born

Early one morning as I was preparing to go to work, I heard Fonda coughing and throwing up in the bathroom. I rushed in to hold her head.

"What's the matter?"

"I don't know. I just feel nauseated."

She wasn't sick. She was expecting our first child. She remained feeling nauseated for about three months, and then she was a bundle of energy. She rushed about the house cleaning, fixing meals, and vacuuming the floors. I was as nervous as a cat taking a bath. I felt like a cat in a fire-ant bed.

Fonda just went about her day as if nothing were happening. As her time to deliver approached, my greatest fear was if I had to deliver the baby myself. At about five on the morning of October 11, 1963, Fonda said she thought it was time to go to the hospital. She said she felt she was ready to have our baby.

I was ready in less than five minutes. Fonda, on the other hand, said she would not go until she fixed her hair and put on her makeup. Two hours later she said we could now go. I didn't need any fingernails trimmed that day. I had already bitten them all off.

I rushed to get Fonda into our Plymouth Valiant. She moved slowly but finally got in. We had a Citizen's Band radio in the car with a long antenna on the back. I unhooked that antenna so that it stood upright on the back

FONDA AT FT KNOX, KENTUCKY, PREGNANT WITH OUR FIRST CHILD

of the car. That was the signal to our neighbors that I was taking Fonda to the hospital to have our baby.

October 11, 1963, Mary Kathryn Marbury (Mitzi), our first child, was born at Ireland Army Hospital in Ft. Knox, Kentucky. I could not see my wife at first but was allowed to see our baby. The baby was in a small bassinet with a pink ribbon attached.

Finally, I saw my wife. I kissed her and asked if the baby was a boy or a girl. The pink ribbon meant nothing to me. She smiled, laughed at my ignorance of what the pink ribbon meant, and told me we had a beautiful baby girl.

The next day when I went to see her at the hospital, the nurses told me that I had to wait to see her until visiting hours. That was about 30 minutes away, and I wanted to see her then. I was the only officer waiting outside the maternity ward, but several enlisted soldiers were also waiting outside. As soon as the nurses left, I opened the door and boldly went in. Everyone else went in also.

There was my wife, looking beautiful with a big grin on her face. I gave her a big kiss and sat beside her on the bed.

"Get off that bed! What do you think this is, the French Riviera!" It was a female nurse who was also a captain in the Army.

"This is my wife," I told her boldly.

"I don't care who she is. Get off that bed."

I did. At least until she left. Then I sat back on the bed again. A few days later we took our daughter home.

Life at Ft. Knox

Our time at Ft. Knox was mostly a happy time. We made many friends. I spent most of the day doing engineering work as the battalion civil engineering officer and Fonda enjoyed time with our daughter and her friends. Fonda and I would play bridge as partners in the evening and enjoy our time together.

RITCHEY & MITZI FONDA & MITZI
FT. KNOX KENTUCKY

Two events did occur during our time at Ft. Knox that created some anxiety. The first was around the middle of 1963. The official dates for the Cuban Missile crisis were between October 16 and 18, 1962, before I even joined the active military. At least that was what was in all the news. What I and most of us at Ft. Knox knew in 1963 was that missiles still existed in Cuba.

Besides being the battalion civil engineering officer, I was also the battalion S2 and S3 officer, meaning I was the battalion intelligence and operations officer. I was, therefore, aware of intelligence information about what was happening in Cuba.

President Kennedy was concerned that the missiles would shortly be used against the United States if something wasn't done. This was near the middle of 1963. While having a routine day at Ft. Knox, I was ordered to report immediately to battalion headquarters.

"Pack up now and be ready to leave for Cuba today."

The army issued me several bandoliers of live ammunition, told me to grab my M1 carbine rifle, pack my battle gear, say goodbye to my wife, and board a train headed for Florida. From there I and the rest of my battalion would be airlifted into Cuba.

The marines and army rangers were to arrive first. I was to arrive shortly afterwards with a few others. After selecting the best place to construct an airfield, the rest of my construction battalion was to arrive a few days later.

I kissed Fonda goodbye and prepared to board the train. Fonda was anxious but ready to do all necessary to take care of our baby while I was gone. She may have been nervous, but she didn't let me see it.

Suddenly all preparations ceased and we were ordered to unpack and return home. The Russians understood the determination of President Kennedy and moved all the missiles out of Cuba, Sadly, a few months later, November 22, 1963, President Kennedy was assassinated.

The second event was near the end of 1964, only a few months before I was to receive my honorable discharge. The Vietnam War was progressing rapidly. Our battalion was issued pith helmets, mosquito netting, and much hot weather gear. The battalion commander called me into his office to ask what I thought was happening. I told him it looked like we were preparing to go to Vietnam. He said there was a rumor that we were going to Alaska.

I told him he must be kidding. He then asked if I would like to extend my time in the Army for another few years. I said if the battalion went to Vietnam before my enlistment period was up, I was ready to go. If not, I was ready to return home and begin my career as a land surveyor and civil engineer.

He again asked what I was planning to tell the others in the battalion if asked where we were likely to be going in the next few months. He told me I must be truthful with any response. I smiled and replied I would say, "My battalion commander told me there was a rumor we were going to Alaska."

"Smart answer," said the battalion commander.

I receive my honorable discharge on January 8, 1965. Three months later my battalion went to Vietnam. I had volunteered for military service and was willing to go anywhere I was ordered during my time in service. Fortunately for me, I never saw combat. Fonda and I prayed often that would happen. Also, fortunately for us, all our close friends eventually came home safely.

CHAPTER SEVEN

Home Again

Heading Home

After cleaning our apartment at Ft. Knox, we headed home. We stopped at Estill Springs, Tennessee, to see Fonda's parents. They had purchased a small home there on top of a hill overlooking the highway. The road into Estill Springs was a narrow two-lane asphalt road. Not much traffic.

We were not sure how to get to Fonda's parents' home, so we stopped at a gas station on the right side of the road. The station was a small concrete block building with one gas pump. It was full service. Full service meant the attendant filled your gas tank rather than you having to do it yourself. It also meant they cleaned your windows, which they did, with a small corn cob.

I asked the station attendant if I could use their telephone.

"Oh, we don't have a telephone, but the store about two blocks down the street is more modern. They even have a telephone and I'm sure they will let you use it."

He smiled as he answered and pointed south.

The store did have a telephone. We used it. Found our way to Fonda's parents' home and enjoyed a short visit. We then continued home to Albany, Georgia.

Home at Last

After a long time on the road, we arrived at my parent's home. They greeted us with hugs and their dog, Bandi, greeted us with a wagging tail. It was good to be home again. My parents had found us a place to rent on Society Avenue, and we proceeded to set up house.

Prices were much lower in 1965 than today in 2026. A gallon of gasoline was $0.31. A medium size new car cost around $2,650, and a Volkswagen Beetle car was $1,595. A dozen eggs were approximately $0.53. The medium annual household income was $6,900 and a new three-bedroom home cost around $21,500. The monthly cost to rent a three-bedroom home was around $118.

You could buy a gallon of milk for around one dollar. Soft drinks were a nickel each and a bar of candy also cost a nickel. Many drug stores sold small pieces of candy for only one penny.

A few months after arriving back to Albany, Georgia, Fonda and I bought our first home. It was a small brick home at 2302 Barnesdale Way, with a fenced in backyard. We loved it.

Fonda decorated the home and then spent most of her time looking after our daughter, Mitzi. I started work with my father at Marbury Engineering Company doing engineering and surveying.

Thanks to my former battalion commander at Ft. Knox writing a recommendation for me to take the surveyor's exam based on experience with the Army Corps of Engineers, I was allowed to take the exam the same year I returned home. I passed the exam on the first try and received my Georgia Land Surveyor's license on December 15, 1965, license number 1495. My next goal was to complete my master's thesis and receive my Master of City Planning (MCP) degree from Georgia Tech.

Fonda's Degree from Georgia Tech

No one could have a better wife than Fonda, especially during those hard-working days. I worked at Marbury Engineering Company two or three days a week. The other days I worked on my thesis. During the day I dictated notes into a reel-to-reel tape recorder. About midnight I finished dictating and woke up Fonda. She then typed on my thesis from the recorder. She finished typing around six in the morning. She then woke me up and I would drive to Georgia Tech, about a three- and one-half hour drive, to meet with my professors.

After meeting with my professors at Georgia Tech, I drove home and dictated again on my thesis. About midnight I would again awaken Fonda, and she typed what I dictated. I again drove the three- and one-half hour drive to Georgia Tech. They reviewed what I had done. I drove home, and the process started over.

Fonda never complained. I would often feel tired and act grumpy. When I did, Fonda just gave me a big kiss, told me she knew I didn't mean to be grumpy, and explained how much she loved me. Sometimes I thought about acting grumpy just to get that kiss.

June 11, 1966, I walked down the aisle at Georgia Tech and received my Master of City Planning degree, but I was not the only one in my family to receive a degree that day. Fonda also received one. She received the MPHE degree, "Mistress of Patience in Husband Engineering."

The diploma was signed by me and E. D. Harrison, president of the Georgia Institute of Technology. The seal at the bottom left corner consisted of a circle, within which were two crossed rolling pins. On the left side of the rolling pins was the initial "M." On the right side was the initial "P." The MP stood for Mistress of Patience.

Her diploma read, "Georgia Institute of Technology. Atlanta, Georgia. This certifies that Fonda Starnes Marbury has continued faithfully to support and encourage a husband through many months of general trials and tribulations, including endless conversations concerning point averages and formulas, numerous harangues delivered fervently on the subject of professional ability, integrity, and idiosyncrasies: countless excuses and attempts at rationalization; infrequent evenings of entertainment; and long hours of burning the midnight oil. By her perseverance she has accomplished the graduation of her husband and is therefore granted this degree of Mistress of Patience in Husband Engineering on this the eleventh day of June nineteen hundred and sixty-six."

Fonda typed more than three thousand pages on a small portable manual typewriter helping with my thesis. She certainly deserved that degree.

Our First Home on Barnesdale Way

As stated earlier, shortly after coming home from the military, and renting a home on Society Avenue, we purchased our first home at 2302 Barnesdale Way. It was only about three blocks from my office.

After receiving my master's degree from Georgia Tech, we now had some time to relax and enjoy life a little more. We usually went on a date every Friday night. We hired a young girl as a babysitter to look after Mitzi.

One evening after returning home and looking for refreshments, we found the refreshments gone. That happened several times again and we suspected they were eaten by our babysitter. We paid her well, and did not mind her eating our food, but we did want her to ask first. Sometimes Fonda prepared refreshments especially for us to eat on returning home. She was frustrated when they were gone.

Since the babysitter did not admit to eating the food, and she obviously thought we did not notice, I had an idea. The babysitter was slightly overweight. Before we

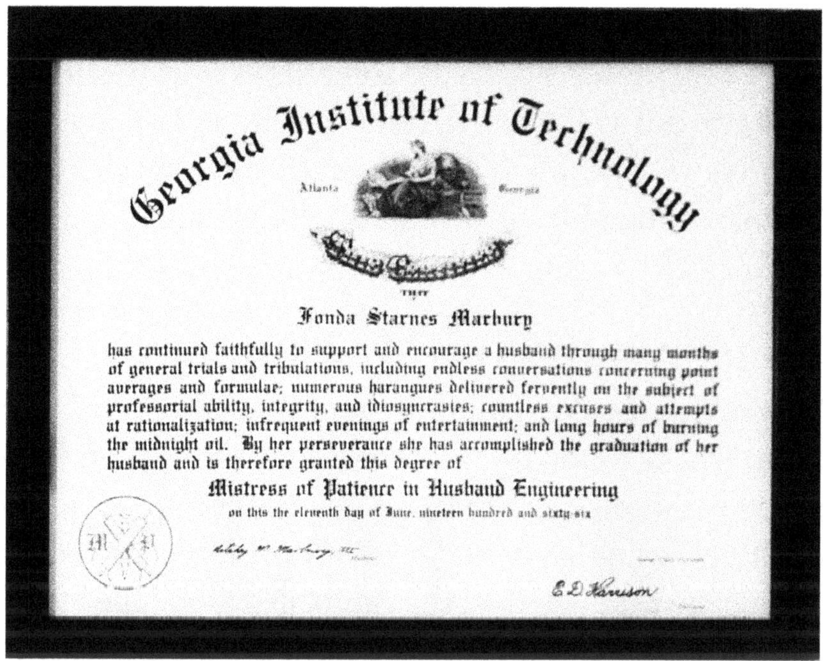

Georgia Institute of Technology

Atlanta Georgia

Fonda Starnes Marbury

has continued faithfully to support and encourage a husband through many months of general trials and tribulations, including endless conversations concerning point averages and formulae; numerous harangues delivered fervently on the subject of professorial ability, integrity, and idiosyncrasies; countless excuses and attempts at rationalization; infrequent evenings of entertainment; and long hours of burning the midnight oil. By her perseverance she has accomplished the graduation of her husband and is therefore granted this degree of

Mistress of Patience in Husband Engineering

on this the eleventh day of June, nineteen hundred and sixty-six

E. D. Harrison

FONDA'S GEORGIA TECH MPHE DEGREE

left for our date one night, I put small pieces of paper on each item of refreshment that Fonda prepared, especially on the sweet stuff.

Some of the notes read, "This food will make you gain weight."

"No. No. No. This food is not for you."

"Be sure to count calories before eating this."

"If this food is gone, we will know who ate it."

When we came home that evening, all the food was still there, and the babysitter had a frown on her face. She could not tell us she found the notes, because that would be admitting she ate the food. We paid her. She took her money and went home.

Never again did we find food and refreshments missing after our dates. Fonda did sometimes fix refreshments for her to eat while we were on our date, but we never again had the problem with her eating the special treats Fonda intended for us to enjoy after our date night.

Camping at two World's Fairs

We were home. We had little money, but we heard there was a World's Fair in New York, and we wanted to go. Hotels were too expensive, so we decided to camp. We purchased a small tent and headed north. We also bought a magazine that listed all the campsites along the way.

Mitzi enjoyed camping. She liked sleeping in the tent with us and had one special fascination. She was fascinated with pit toilets. Fonda and I enjoyed the scenery, the lakes, the mountains, and the flowers you could see that were often planted beside the road. Mitzi, however, enjoyed the pit toilets best.

When we finally arrived in New York, we found a spot to camp and went directly to the World's Fair. It was fascinating. Rides were everywhere. Exhibits were everywhere, and people of all nationalities were there.

One special exhibit was the premier showing of Walt Disney's "It's a Small World." It featured animated children from all over the world, dressed in native costumes, singing and dancing as we watched them from a boat that floated around the exhibit inside a huge pavilion.

We heard music all over the park. Mitzi loved it. In fact, she loved it so much that she started dancing in the street. She was only two, but always active. She was so active that we had to tie a rope around her waist to keep her from running away. She soon became the main attraction. Crowds gathered just to see her dancing in the street.

Meals were expensive, at least to us. Once at the fair Fonda bought a meal and later found it cost five dollars. She cried because of the high cost. Five dollars in those days was a lot of money.

Two years later we found that the World's Fair, Expo 67, would be in Montreal, Canada. We wanted to go. We again packed our tent and took off for Canada. The drive took about 20 hours, or two days. At that time no visa or passport was required to go in and out of the country. We just drove to the border, gave our name to the border guard, and proceeded to the World's Fair.

We found a campsite near the fair, pitched our tent, and settled in for the evening. Once our tent was ready, we called Mitzi for supper. She was not there. We looked everywhere, but she was nowhere to be found. It was getting dark and around us were nothing but tents. Several campsites had fires going, and we walked to every campsite. No Mitzi. Finally, one campsite had several children sitting around the campfire. Mitzi was one of them.

Mitzi had walked off, found a friend, and proceeded to sit down by their fire and play. Once we found Mitzi,

MITZI, FONDA & POP TENT

we apologized for her imposing on their family. They just laughed and said they expected her parents would show up soon.

The next day we visited Montreal. A very kind local man showed us around the city, and we had a fun time. I visited the local Rotary Club while there. A few days later we returned home. Our cost for the entire one-week trip was only $87, including gas for the car.

Our Second Child

"Mitzi," asked Fonda, "How would you like to have a little sister or a little brother?"

We were still in our Barnesdale Way home and Fonda was to have another baby. I was delighted.

Mitzi felt fine about having a sister, but reluctant about having a brother. After some deliberation she finally said, "A little brother will be OK if you name him Sweet Pea." Swee 'Pea was the name of Popeye's adopted son. Popeye the Sailorman was a popular cartoon of the day.

Sure enough, Mitzi would shortly have a little brother. We would name him after my grandfather, father, and me, Ritchey McGuire Marbury, IV. His nickname would be Rick.

Like with our first child, I was as nervous as a lamb in a lion's den. Fonda, as usual, however, was concerned about her makeup.

I said, "Let's go."

She said, "I have to fix my hair."

I said, "Hurry. I don't want to deliver this baby."

Fonda said, "We have plenty of time."

We didn't. Our little boy arrived shortly after we got to Phoebe Putney Memorial Hospital in Albany, Georgia.

It was almost Christmas when Rick was born, December 23, 1967. Fonda was allowed to go home, but in those days newborn babies had to stay in the hospital longer. We would spend that Christmas with Mitzi, but Rick would have to stay in the hospital. Every year he continues to remind us that we left him alone on his first Christmas.

Home on Green Valley Lane

Fonda wanted her dream home. It was to be a home on a hill, along a street with little traffic, and in a subdivision I personally designed. She wanted lots of bathrooms, lots of storage space, large walk-in closets, and a large kitchen. We decided to sell our home on Barnesdale Way, purchase a lot on Green Valley Lane, and hire a contractor to build Fonda's dream home.

There were two problems with buying the lot on Green Valley. One was that we had very little money, so we could not afford to buy the lot. Fonda helped by teaching piano lessons. The other was that the lot was on a flat piece of land, not on a hill.

The lot was owned by Walden and Kirkland Realtors, one of our major clients. I was the engineer doing the subdivision design. Besides being our client, the owners were good friends. They wanted us to live there, so they worked with us to help us afford to buy the lot. They agreed to allow us to pay them only fifty dollars a month for the lot.

Next, we had to sell our Barnesdale home before moving. It sold quickly, much more quickly than we expected. Now we had to find a place to live until our home on Green Valley was constructed. The contractor, Billups Johnson, was also a friend. He owned an apartment complex and agreed to let us rent one of his apartments until he completed construction on our new home.

The banker was also a friend and helped us get a home

HOME ON GREEN VALLEY LANE

loan at the lowest interest rate allowed at that time. The result was that our house payment was only $119 a month. Our home would be a little over 1800 square feet on an acre lot in one of the best locations in Albany, Georgia.

The help of so many friends helped us conquer our first problem, how to pay for the home. Fonda had the solution for the second problem, how to have a house on a hill. Since I was the engineer designing the subdivision, she told me to just lower the street four feet.

I said, "Fonda, you have got to be kidding."

She said, "No, all you have to do to create me a hill is to lower the street four feet."

Fonda always had a way of making things seem simple, whether they were or not. I thought about it and said, "Why not?" I lowered the street four feet.

The good thing about lowering the street was that the low-lying lots at the end of the street, originally too low to build on, became buildable and desirable. The reason, dirt removed by lowering the street provided enough material to fill the low-lying lots and make them usable.

We moved into our dream home in 1968. The address, 1824 Green Valley Lane, Albany, Georgia 31707. This was to be our forever home, or so we thought.

CHAPTER EIGHT

Joining the Church of Jesus Christ of Latter-Day Saints

Baptism and Temple Sealing

Fonda and I were baptized into The Church of Jesus Christ of Latter-day Saints on September 4, 1969. I won't discuss our conversion story here because it is covered in the book by Hartman Rector, Jr. The book is titled *No More Strangers: Volume 2*. Suffice it to say we studied the Church for eight years before deciding to join. We lost no friends when we joined and still have many friends, both members of our new church, members of other churches, and members of no church. Fonda and I both believe individuals should do what they believe is right. We will not always agree, but we can always care about one another and continue to be friends regardless of our beliefs.

Fonda and I deeply love each other and always felt and wished we could be together for eternity. Now we

Marriage Certificate

This Certifies that

RITCHEY MCGUIRE MARBURY III and FONDA GAYLE STARNES

Who were previously legally married on 16, JUNE 1962,
at ALBANY, GEORGIA, were Sealed by me as husband and wife
according to the ordinance of God, for Time and for all Eternity,
in the House of the Lord, at SALT LAKE CITY, UTAH, 16, JUNE 1971.

Witnesses

An Elder of the Church of Jesus Christ of Latter-day Saints

TEMPLE MARRIAGE CERTIFICATE

learned that it was possible and we arranged to go to the Salt Lake Temple in Salt Lake City, Utah, to be sealed for time and all eternity. Harold B. Lee, the current president of the quorum of the twelve apostles and later president of the Church performed the sealing. The date was June 16, 1971. Charlie Sellers and Glen Rudd were the two witnesses. Charlie had baptized us, and Glen Rudd was the mission president that spent much time teaching us before we joined.

David and Connie Kammer

One couple, not mentioned in the book, *No More Strangers Volume 2*, was David and Connie Kammer. David was my roommate in college and also a groomsman when Fonda and I were married in the Methodist Church in Albany, Georgia. They joined The Church of Jesus Christ of Latter-day Saints in April 1969, just five months before us. Before joining, neither of us knew either was interested in that Church, even though David and I were close friends.

David was immaculate in organizing and keeping things clean and neat. He was also creative and always doing unusual things. Fonda and I would often visit David and Connie in their home in Chattanooga, Tennessee.

David and I were both airplane pilots. On one visit David was constructing a helicopter using only materials he ordered and put together himself. He proudly showed Fonda and me his helicopter and how he would soon test it out. The helicopter was anchored to the ground with metal anchors tied to a concrete pad. Straps secured the metal anchors to the helicopter.

Finely it was time to test the helicopter. David jumped into the cockpit and started the engine. It roared to a start and lifted off the ground. Without warning, one of the straps broke. The helicopter leaned forward crashing the nose of the helicopter into the concrete below. That was the last time he worked on the helicopter. He never finished it and never got to fly it, other than his test flight that ended in a crash. Still, the fact that David could construct a helicopter from scratch is testimony to his talents.

After both of our families joined the Church, we studied Church History. Both of us were fascinated with how Church members crossed the Mississippi River. David decided to try that himself. He just proceeded to swim across the Mississippi on one of their trips to Nauvoo. Probably foolish, but that was David, always trying what most people never dared.

After joining the Church, David and Connie served a mission in Russia. Fonda and I served a mission in Idaho.

Chickenpox

A year after Fonda and I joined the Church of Jesus Christ of Latter-day Saints, we received our patriarchal blessing. That was on September 8, 1970. This is a blessing offering inspired guidance and counsel. It is considered a spiritual "roadmap" for one's life. My blessing was a very comforting one offering encouragement whenever I encountered difficult situations.

There was one part of the blessing I did not understand, however. The blessing told me to read the book of Job in the Bible. I had read it before, but I read it again after the blessing. It told how Job remained faithful to his Heavenly Father even after undergoing numerous trials and disappointments. One of those trials included Job receiving painful boils from the sole of his foot to the crown of his head. I did not expect that to happen to me, but it did.

One morning I woke up with painful sores along the bottom of my feet. During the next few days the sores covered my entire body with painful boils from the bottom of my feet to the top of my head, including boils inside my mouth. I don't remember ever feeling so sick. I had chickenpox.

Fonda had begun teaching piano lessons while I served in the military. She continued that after we got home and after our baptism into the Church. Fortunately, Fonda stayed healthy and was able to continue teaching piano lessons even though I was very sick. She looked after me and did all she could to make me comfortable. It's amazing she even stayed in the same house with me. With all the boils on my face I looked like "the creature from the Black Lagoon."

One afternoon she needed to go to the store to purchase some food and medicine. A piano student was due at our home later that day, but Fonda assured me she would be home in time to teach the piano lesson. She wasn't. Before she returned, the doorbell rang. I hesitated to go to the door, but knowing her student was due to arrive, I did.

I opened the door. Fonda's piano student took one look at me and started screaming. I backed off. She screamed some more. The boils all over my face had turned into large red blisters causing me to look scarier than any monster on television or in the movies.

Thankfully, Fonda arrived almost at the same time. I

rushed to my bedroom and hid. Fonda somehow managed to calm her student down and give her the scheduled piano lesson. Fortunately, no one ever contracted chickenpox from me, and I recovered in a few months. We both laugh about that situation now, but it sure was not funny then.

Flying Airplanes

During my early years as a member of the church, I also had a private pilot's license. I would often take our plane to Orlando, Florida, for business. On one trip our son, Rick, wanted to fly with me. After a brief chat with Fonda, she agreed, and took Rick to the airport to meet me.

Another friend was also flying with me that day. He was a rather large man weighing close to 300 pounds. As Fonda took Rick to the plane, Rick took one look at the large man, looked over at Fonda, and then looked at me.

"Is that man flying with us?"

"He sure is," I said. "I told him last week he could fly with me."

"Then I am not going," said Rick. "That man is so heavy that the plane will not get off the ground, and if it does it will surely go back down and crash. If he goes, I'm not going."

Embarrassed, Fonda took Rick back home.

All my experiences flying airplanes are too numerous to mention, but one is especially worth noting. It is when I flew Fonda to Estill Springs, Tennessee, to visit her parents. It was a bright, sunny day, a perfect day for flying except for high winds. The wind that day was blowing at 40 miles per hour.

My plane was a small, single-engine, Cessna Cardinal. Fonda was always nervous about flying, but the trip took five hours by car and less than two hours by plane. Reluctantly Fonda agreed to go since the weather was clear. She did not think about the high winds. Our plan was to land the plane in Tullahoma, Tennessee. Her parents would pick us up from there and drive us to their home in Estill Springs.

The flight to Tullahoma was uneventful until it was time to land. The wind was blowing straight down the runway so I felt landing there would be a simple thing. It was, except for one problem. The stall speed on my airplane was 37 mph, and the headwind was 40 mph. The more I tried to land the plane the more it just hovered motionless above the airport.

Fonda was terrified and felt sure we were going to crash. I told Fonda we couldn't be safer since the plane was hardly moving. That did not satisfy Fonda. Finally, I was able to land the plane on the runway under conditions few pilots ever experience. Since the headwind was 40 miles per hour and my airplane stall speed was 37 miles per hour, when I touched down on the runway, my plane was actually going backwards at a groundspeed of 3 miles per hour.

Fonda was so frightened that she almost refused to fly back home with me. In fact, she required me to place a small empty can in the airplane with us just in case she had to go to the bathroom on the flight home.

Called to Serve: Idaho Pocatello/Idaho Boise Mission

It was early afternoon on Friday, February 10, 1978. I arrived home to see my family gleaming with excitement.

"Guess what, daddy?" asked Mizi.

"Did Fluffy have kittens?" I answered. Fluffy was our cat.

"Yes," said Mitzi, "On your pillow!"

After a few laughs, Fonda told me I had received a call from Marion G. Romney, a member of the first presidency of the Church. When Fonda explained I was not home, his secretary said he would call back around 6:30.

At 6:30 I answered the phone to hear President Romney.

"This is a preliminary call," he said. "If you were called to preside over one of the missions of the Church, would you accept?"

I said I would gladly do anything the Lord requested of me.

President Romney then proceeded to interview me. The interview was brief and very specific regarding my worthiness. After the interview President Romney said I would know if I was to be called in about a week or two. I didn't know if I passed or failed the interview. Mitzi was especially excited, but we did not tell Rick. We reminded Mitzi not to tell anyone.

The following Sunday afternoon, February 12, I asked David Hanna, a close friend, to give me a priesthood blessing that I might be prepared to do whatever the Lord requested of me. I did not tell him of my call from President Romney. In the blessing I was promised the spiritual strength needed to do whatever the Lord requested of me. It was a very spiritual experience for both of us.

February 21, 1978, I received a letter from the Church Missionary Department signed by Spencer W. Kimball, president of the Church of Jesus Christ of Latter-day Saints. It was also signed by N. Eldon Tanner, his first counselor, and by Marion G. Romney, his second counselor. The letter said I was to preside over one of the missions of the Church. The name of the mission would be given to me later. My wife, Fonda, was also called as my companion. I could expect to assume the presidency approximately July 1, 1978.

When I told my father I would be leaving for three years to serve a mission for my Church, he was unhappy. He said that was too much of a sacrifice and that I would lose my home and my business. I understood that was true but also understood that doing what the Lord asks is more important.

We let Mitzi tell Rick about our call, and we told him not to let anyone know. John Fowler, a friend, came to our home about 30 minutes later and Rick promptly told him. Rick was just too excited not to tell.

On March 4, 1978, Fonda and I wrote a letter accepting our call to serve. It went as follows:

Dear Brethren:

It is with deep humility and a keen desire to serve our Heavenly Father that my wife and I accept this call to preside over one of the missions of the Church of Jesus Christ of Latter-day Saints.

We understand our responsibilities and commit ourselves to complete obedience and service. We will seek the guidance of our Heavenly Father in all that we do and endeavor to bring honor and glory to His kingdom.

Sincerely,
Ritchey M. Marbury, III
Fonda Marbury

We soon learned we would serve in the Idaho Pocatello Mission.

Now we prepared to leave. The Church had a maximum amount of items and a maximum weight we could take with us, so we had to dispose of much.

We picked up our boat from Lake Seminole in Bainbridge, Georgia, and took it to Huggins Outboard Motor Company to have them sell it for us. We had a garage sale to get rid of other items we could not take with us. Friends agreed to keep much of our furniture. We arranged with

Walden and Kirkland Realtors to rent our home. We also sold our car.

Next, we flew to Provo, Utah, to attend the Language Training Mission Home at Brigham Young University. Training began on Monday, June 19, 1978. Elder Carlos E. Asay conducted most of the training. Elder Thomas S. Monson introduced all of the mission presidents and their wives.

At 3:30 p.m. on June 22, 1978, Fonda and I were set apart for our mission. Elder Boyd K. Packer set me apart and Elder Hugh W. Pinnock set apart my wife, Fonda. Elder Packer was a member of the quorum of the twelve apostles and Elder Pinnock was a member of the first quorum of the seventy.

After completing the five-day training, we flew back home to Albany, Georgia. Then on Tuesday, June 27, we again left Albany, Georgia, for Salt Lake City. Our ten-year-old son, Rick, and our fourteen-year-old daughter, Mitzi, flew with us. We arrived in Salt Lake City that night and flew to Pocatello, Idaho, the following Thursday.

Mission Begins

Shortly before noon on June 29, 1978, Fonda and I with our two children arrived in Pocatello, Idaho. The current mission president, Sherman M. Crump, met us at the airport along with his two assistants, Elders Raymond Roberge and Ronald Jewett. President Crump took us to our new home at 5055 Mohawk, introduced us to his wife, fed us, discussed the mission with us for about an hour, and left. Fonda and I were now in charge of a mission with 61 stakes and 142 missionaries.

The boundaries went from Pendleton, Oregon, on the west; Yellowstone National Park and Jackson, Wyoming, on the east; Jackpot, Nevada, on the south; and most of Idaho on the north and interior of the mission. The mission boundaries did not include the northern panhandle of Idaho.

I wanted to meet all the missionaries as soon as possible, so shortly after arriving I schedule a plane trip from Pocatello to Boise. Fonda took me to the airport and watched as I boarded the plane. The engine started, the plane taxied down the runway, and then completely off the runway. Dust spewed everywhere and the plane came to an abrupt stop. Fonda just calmly watched as the passengers and I departed that plane and walked over to another. After boarding, the flight to Boise and back was uneventful. I must confess, however, I was a little concerned with airplane flight safety for the next few months.

My next task was to call two counselors. I called a dentist, Dr. Robert E. Lee, as my first counselor and a seminary teacher, Erwin Wirkus as my second counselor. President Lee was a skilled photographer and took many pictures of the mission. He prepared an album showing pictures of all the missionaries that served in the mission about the time that Fonda and I were released from service.

President Wirkus was not only my second counselor, but he was also the former mission president of the

Vienna Austria and Des Moines Iowa Missions. He also published the book, *Judge Me Dear Reader,* about Emma Smith, the wife of Joseph Smith, Jr.

We spend the next few days meeting the missionaries and conducting zone conferences. One family took us to a Rodeo on the evening of July third. We were southerners. July temperatures were in the eighties and nineties back home. We wore light clothing with short sleeve shirts. Pocatello was different. Temperatures were below freezing that evening.

"Does it ever get summer here in Pocatello?" I asked our host family.

"Oh yes," they replied. "Summer came on a Thursday last year."

Yes, Pocatello was in a very cold location. The temperature was often below zero. The average temperature in January, 1979, was 10.5 degrees Fahrenheit. It took some time for Fonda and me to get used to it. I remember one day that first winter in 1979 we went to visit missionaries in Jackson Hole, Wyoming. The temperature (not wind child, but the actual temperature) was 50 degrees below zero. You could literally spit, and it would freeze almost as soon as it hit the ground.

As mission president I received a living allowance to cover basic needs, including a home to live in, a stipend to cover basic personal living expenses, and some health care services. Dental care was not covered. Unlike most of the mission presidents during that period, that living allowance was our only source of income. Lucky for us, my first counselor, Dr. Lee, was a dentist and performed all our needed dental work at no cost.

I am really grateful for Dr. Lee. In October, 1979, he found five cavities and did what was necessary to correct the problem. I am not sure how I reacted to the drilling and his working on my teeth, but I hope I did not act too badly. Dr. Lee told me he could tell the character of a person by how they acted at the dentist.

Years later, after returning from my mission, I wrote a sonnet about a visit to the dentist. Here it is:

I Went to See My Dentist

I went to see my dentist yesterday.
I must admit it scared me just to think
Of how much it would hurt and what I'd pay
To hear that drill and hear his work tools clink.
He stuffed my mouth with cotton swabs and then
He asked if I was comfortable, and well,
Of course I couldn't talk, just simply grin
And hope I wouldn't jump or scream or yell.
He stuck some pointed tools between my lips.
He scraped my teeth and poked around my gums.
His tools all had bright shiny pointed tips.
His drill made grinding high pitched scary hums.
When done, he said I was completely fit.
And I said, "Wow, it didn't hurt a bit!"

On our first Christmas in the mission field, Fonda and I could only spend five dollars on Christmas presents for each other. I bought Fonda a comb and an "Ugly Purple Scarf." She eventually lost the comb, but many years later she was still using that "Ugly Purple Scarf" to cover her hair as she was dressing.

Ricks College had me speak at one of their meetings and offered to pay me, which I refused. Of course I would not take the money. A month or so later, David and Charlee Hanna, friends from Albany, Georgia, came to visit. They brought us some food which we were very thankful for. They probably had no idea that we were living on such a small income. When they left, we noticed the price tag for the food was still in the grocery bag. When we looked, we saw that what they paid for the food was almost the exact same amount that Ricks College had offered to pay us.

In those days missionaries lived on what little income they, their parents, or others had saved to finance their missions. This was usually around one hundred to one hundred fifty dollars a month, a small amount even in the late nineteen seventies.

One missionary was supported only by his mother whose income was barely enough to support herself, let alone her son. I later discovered he was only eating one meal a day. The story of how prayer provided the additional income is found in my book, *Dear Missionaries Volume 2*, so I will not discuss it here. Suffice it to say that after fervent prayer, a generous benefactor learned of his need and provided full support for the rest of his mission.

Around the first part of July 1979, the mission headquarters moved Pocatello to Boise, Idaho. The new mission home address was 4981 Umatilla, Boise, Idaho 83709. The address of the new mission office became 182 South Cole Road, Boise, Idaho 83709. The name of the mission changed from the Idaho Pocatello Mission to the Idaho Boise Mission.

A few months before the move, several missionaries worked on the new mission office to prepare it for the move. Their work included adjusting workspaces and walls to create different rooms within the office

Every week the missionaries wrote a letter to me, and I also wrote a letter to them, as well as a monthly letter to all stake and ward missionaries. Those letters are published in my first book, *Dear Missionaries*.

Fonda and I also had many spiritual experiences during our mission. Many of those experiences are in my book, *Dear Missionaries Volume 2*. For that reason, I will not discuss most of them here.

Asthma

Fonda and I had only been on our mission for a little more than three months when I had trouble breathing. The high altitude and cold weather were not what a South Georgia boy was used to. I could breathe out, but when I tried to breathe back in, I couldn't. It was like someone was holding my chest to keep it from moving. I could not take deep breaths. I would gasp for air. I would wheeze and then cough.

A little over a year later the asthma continued to get worse. On August 24, 1979, I went to an asthma specialist, Dr. Michael Ganier. I had no idea what was going to happen next. To test for allergies, he stuck my back with needles, about fifty pin pricks. I expected one or two, but fifty? I felt like a pin cushion. The tests indicated I was allergic to cats and house dust. He gave me some medicine and told me to report its effect in a week or two.

The medicine was 250 milligrams of anhydrous theophylline, trade name, Elixophyllin, taken twice daily. Symptoms from the medicine were worse than the asthma. It made my stomach upset and me grouchy. I couldn't even jog a minute and one half or play a full game of ping pong without having an asthma attack. Every day it got harder to breathe. Doctors wanted me to go home. To me that was not an option.

One year later, and after some research I decided to try vitamins. They could not be any worse than the medicine. The medicine did no good and made me feel terrible.

I started taking 500 milligrams of vitamin C three times daily and 100 milligrams of vitamin B6 twice daily. It helped. Soon I could jog for almost two minutes. Not much, but progress. By the end of our mission, I was doing fine with almost no sign of asthma.

Embarrassing Moments

I wish I could say things always went smoothly for us, but that would not be true. Life always has its embarrassing moments. That was true while holding a meeting with missionaries in the Rexburg, Idaho, area in August, 1980. It was a very spiritual meeting. All at the meeting felt inspired. We closed with a prayer.

After kneeling for the prayer, we stood up. A ripping sound broke the silence. All but Fonda were standing.

"Get up Fonda," I whispered.

Red-faced, she tried to stand, but a louder rip pierced the silence. I looked down to see what I thought was a white string attached to her shoe.

"Stand up and I'll get it off," I whispered again.

Another loud rit. Now I was red-faced. That string was the hem of Fonda's slip. It was caught in the heal of her shoe. Full of as much grace and charm as possible, Fonda excused herself, went to the restroom, and cut off the hem. We then proceeded to our next appointment.

April 8, 1981, was another of those embarrassing moments. Elder Waldie, a full time Idaho missionary, and I were making our way down Franklin Street in Boise, Idaho. We were riding in a new, three-week-old blue Chevy Citation, the one provided to me to use as mission president, when we stopped for a red light. A Chevrolet truck stopped just in front of us.

The light changed green and the truck moved ahead

slowly in a right turn. I followed, continuing straight down Franklin.

Then it happened. A young boy stepped in front of the truck. The truck driver slammed on the brakes, and the truck stopped several yards in front of the boy. In the meanwhile, seeing the light had changed and the truck ahead was moving forward, I glanced in the rearview mirror for about one second. That was the wrong second.

"Look out!" Shouted Elder Waldie. It was too late. I quickly applied the brakes, but not soon enough. One embarrassing thud later I was guilty of being responsible for one of those "preventable" accidents I had been lecturing the office staff about.

When I returned my car to the office to make out the accident report and arrange for repairs, I asked Elder Tatham for the keys to another car. He handed me the keys to a white Chevy Nova. I took them and left the office to drive home.

As I started to drive out of the parking lot, I noticed a small handwritten note on the glove compartment. Surely the office staff didn't have time to place it there before I took the car. The note read, "No one goes far just looking into the rearview mirror!"

Apartment Inspections

Fonda and I routinely inspected missionary apartments. To us it was important that missionaries kept neat, clean, and healthy apartments. The missionaries did not always like us doing that, but they never complained. Fonda later wrote a poem about apartment inspections. Here it is:

PICK UP YOUR SOX

Written by my wife, Fonda Marbury, to young missionaries, after visiting their apartments. The initials, "DA" stand for Dinner Appointment.

Pick up your sox and make your bed,
Then set your table–so bountifully spread.
Wash your dishes all shiny and bright–
Mold discourages the appetite.
Wash yourself all clean and spiffy–
A shower a day takes only a jiffy.
At a DA, please be polite-
Stay only one hour and not all night.
Use your very best manners you strong and able–
And get those elbows off the table.
Every Monday without fail,
Clean your floors with mop and pail.
Wash your car. Wash your clothes.
Change your sheets–goodness knows!
Clean the bathroom, and the doors.
Write your letters, do your chores.
Always remember who you are–

You may be someone's shining star.
If you are always faithful and true,
Your Heavenly Father will be proud of you.

Paper Routes

During our mission, once we moved to Boise, Mitzi and Rick had paper routes. They had to leave home around 5:00 in the morning to have the papers delivered not later than 6:30. Early every morning, a stack of papers had to be picked up at a separate location. The stack was then taken home. Each paper had to be rolled into a small bundle that could be tossed to the home front door of the paper subscribers. Fonda became an expert at rolling newspapers. She could roll two newspapers for every one newspaper rolled by me, Mitzi, or Rick.

There was one main drawback to the paper routes. Although the children and I found it hard to get up that early each morning to prepare and deliver papers, Fonda loved it. Even after we returned home from our mission, Fonda wanted Mitzi and Rick to get paper routes so that she could help them again with their routes. Thankfully, I finally persuaded her not to do so.

Mission Spiritual Experiences

The mission provided many spiritual experiences. I feel some of them need to be discussed here, even though they are discussed in a previous book. The experiences mentioned below are found in my book, *Dear Missionaries, Volume 2*. It is a transcript of a talk I gave while serving in Idaho. The title, "Why Me?"

Not long after I came out on my mission, we had a missionary arrive.The missionary told me the story of his father, and how he came out on his mission. His father had a very rare disease called Myasthenia Gravis. Many of you have never heard of that disease. It is so rare that many doctors feel that if they treat three or four patients, they have had a great deal of experience. Extremely rare. It's a disease of the muscles that causes you to have absolutely no control over your body movement.The man that had this disease, this young man' s father, couldn't raise his arms; he couldn't move his legs. He even had difficulty holding his eyelids open. That's how serious the disease was.

He couldn't move his neck, and he had to wear a neck brace. He couldn't swallow because he didn't even have control of the muscles that allow him to swallow. He couldn't speak, although he could mumble enough to communicate, but very unintelligibly. It was very difficult to understand him.

This man, of course, wasn't able to earn the income necessary to send his son on a mission, but his son wanted to go. The Bishop wanted him to be able to go.

After prayer, the Bishop came to this man and said, "Brother, we have a calling for you in the Church. Of course, the young man's father looked at him questioningly, and then the answer was, "The calling that we have for you is to be Assistant Ward Clerk."

The young man's father forced as much of a smile as he could , thinking to himself, "Now isn't that silly! Here I am, I can't even move my fingers. I can't even swallow, and they're calling me to be Assistant Ward Clerk. A job that requires me to be able to see and I can't hold by eyelids open. A job that requires me to have at least enough manual dexterity to be able to write numbers and add them back and forth. There's no way I can do it."

The Bishop said again, "Brother So and So, we're calling you to be the Assistant Ward Clerk, and this is a call from the Lord."

The missionary related to me how his father explained that he remembered how his Patriarchial Blessing promised if he would accept any calling that he received, that the Lord would bless him to the extent that he would be able to fulfill that calling. He thought to himself, "Well, I don't know how much faith I really have, but if I accept it, the Lord has to heal me for me to be able to act as an Assistant Ward Clerk. I really can't lose anything. I don't like the idea of being a Clerk. If I had my druthers, I think the last calling I'd want in the Church would be that of a Clerk."

Then he thought, "I'll do it. I'll put the Lord to the test."

He indicated to the Bishop as best he could that he would accept the call.

Then the Bishop did something. The Bishop exercised faith. I wonder how many Bishops have this much faith. The Bishop said, "I also feel impressed that I should give you a blessing. Will it be alright?"

The man nodded yes. The Bishop then put his hands on the head of that father, and said, "By the authority of the Priesthood which I hold, and in the name of Jesus Christ, I command your body to be made whole."

Now here's a man that's dying. Myasthenia Gravis is a disease for which there is no cure. Here is a Bishop talking to a man that has been told by all the competent medical authorities in the area that he was going to die. The Bishop commands this man's body to be made whole and promises him health. Then he leaves.

I learned the rest of that story shortly after the son was on his mission. I received a phone call, and it was from the young man's father. I had heard this story, so I told the man, "I'm surprised to hear you are able to speak. Your son told me that you had Myasthenia.
I had a friend that died of that disease."

I didn't mean to discourage him, but sometimes your choice of words is not what it should be. I asked, Well, how are you doing? How are you feeling?"

He replied , "I can best answer that by telling you that I'm a barber. (That requires some manual dexterity.) My business is going so well that I've just opened a second business."

"In other words, you are cured?"

"Yes," he said." It didn't happen all at once. I accepted the call, and suddenly I found that I could make every meeting and I was able to be an Assistant Ward Clerk. I found that all of a sudden I was getting better."

Then he said, "I didn't really realize exactly what had happened and the extent of the blessings. so I quit going to church for a little while. You know, I was back in bed again. I repented of that, and went back to my calling as Assistant Ward Clerk and I haven't had any problems since."

I said , "I'll bet you haven't missed any meetings since either, have you?" Of course, his answer was, "I sure haven't! " (Note: I saw this man's son again in October, 2016. The son told me his father was still alive and doing well.)

You see what can happen when you are really prepared? When you are spiritually in tune as this Bishop was, you can demonstrate the power of God by your actions.

This Bishop, when the Lord gave him a message, acted on it. He knew what it meant to pray. He understood how to be receptive to prayer. This Bishop, in answer to a commandment from the Lord, walked over to a dying man and commanded his body to be made whole, and it happened. It happened because that Bishop said, "Why not me?" rather than "Why me?"

Another example happened about a year ago. Two missionaries were teaching a young lady—probably in her middle twenties. She was expecting a baby and she had a very serious concern. She had been told by her doctor that she had cancer and there was concern whether or not she would live. Even more serious than that, there was concern on the part of this lady whether or not her yet-to-be-born baby would live.

The lady expressed that her concern wasn't nearly so much for her own life as for the life of her unborn baby. During the process of the discussions, the missionaries taught how the apostles of old were able to give blessings and people were restored to health.

The lady said, "If the apostles of old could do it and this is the true Church and you represent the Savior, why can't you cure me?"

She asked in faith for these two missionaries to give her a blessing. They did. Then they left. The next day, the lady went to the hospital. She was examined again to see how far the cancer had progressed and to set a date for an operation. After the examination, the doctor said, "I don't understand it. Somehow in the last few days, a miracle has occurred . Your cancer has reversed itself. It is now smaller than the head of a pin. We can probably do nothing and it will simply go away. If you would like, we can operate, but now it is so small that it will be a minor operation. In fact, so minor that we can assure you good health. We can also assure your baby to be born in good health."

The example I just gave you occurred in the east end of this mission . Another example—over in the west end of the mission. A missionary, this time going out with a team teacher, was over in an area visiting a man to teach him about the Gospel. They asked him to be baptized , and the man said that he wouldn't be able to; that he probably wouldn't live that long.

It was explained to the missionaries that this man, also, had cancer, but it was much more serious. The man had a cancerous growth behind his left ear . It was growing so rapidly, and it was so serious, that the man had already obtained total blindness in his left eye and partial blindness in his right eye. The doctor's expectation was that this man would not live more than two weeks. There was, however, a specialist in Portland, Oregon, who could perhaps perform an operation that would extend his life for a few months so that he could get his affairs in order.

In order to keep the man's hopes from getting too high, they explained very frankly that there was no way that his life could be saved—the cancer had gone too far. He would die, but perhaps they could extend his life a month or two. The man was preparing to leave the next day to go for the emergency operation when the missionaries were there. They taught him, and they also explained the principles of faith. They explained the power of commitment and how the Lord blesses those who are sincere. They asked him if he wanted to be baptized, and he said yes, but he felt he needed to go for the operation first and he didn't know if he would make it back. He then asked for a blessing.

Now listen to this. Here's a man who is literally dying of a disease just as deadly—in fact, more deadly—than the leprosy that we hear about all through the scriptures.

Here's a man who has cancer so far progressed that he is blind in his left eye and partially blind in his right eye. This missionary and his team teacher laid their hands on the head of this man, and the missionary sealed the blessing, saying, "By the power of the Holy Priesthood which we hold, and in the name of Jesus Christ, we command your body to be made whole." Then they left .

The next morning when the man awoke to get ready for his trip, he knew something was different. Not only was his vision now perfect in his right eye, which had been partially blind, but he also was able to see out of his left eye. His vision had been restored. He didn't understand it, but he knew that there was something that was happening within his body and he felt better.

He left and was rushed to the specialist in Portland, Oregon. The specialist observed him, then others were probably brought in. After some deliberation, they told the man they wanted to have a conference with him. The doctor said, "We don't understand it. A miracle has occurred. The cancer in your body has died. Not only that, you're well. You're cured. We haven't done anything. We don't know what happened, except we know that you're cured. You go back home and live a good life and just thank the Lord for your blessings."

He went back, and as you can imagine, he was baptized just a few days later.

The point is, here were some missionaries who were working hard, were dedicated, had prepared themselves spiritually, as well as mentally, emotionally, and physically, and were not afraid to demonstrate the power of the Lord. Here were some missionaries who lived so close to their Heavenly Father that they were able to read the scriptures, and to exhibit the same faith as the prophets of old who had performed miracles.

They didn't say, "Why me?" They simply said, "Why not me?" They demonstrated the power of the Lord, and received the blessings that come from having faith and living a proper life.

Another example. I told this to the missionaries not too long ago. We had two missionaries who were very concerned about the people that they could bring into the Gospel. They had taught the Gospel to a number of people, but were not having any success. The people weren't accepting the messages as they felt they should. So the missionaries said , "Alright, we'll prepare ourselves through prayer and fasting."

This incident happened on February 17. They fasted, knelt down, prayed and asked the Lord to bless them by putting them in contact with someone who was ready to hear the message they were about to present. After fasting for the noon and evening meals, they went to sleep.

At 3:00 a.m., the phone rang. It was a Bishop on the other end of the line saying that someone had called the hot line and asked to speak to some ministers, preferably missionaries. By 3:30 a.m., the missionaries were teaching the individual.

They taught him for a while, went back home and got a couple hours' sleep, then went back. They met with him around 8:00 that morning and for five hours they continued to teach him the principles of the Gospel. Seven days later, February 24, that individual was baptized.

I told about that incident at our last zone conference in Twin Falls. This morning I received a phone call from a missionary over in Twin Falls, and he said, "President Marbury, do you remember telling us about what happened to the missionaries who prayed and fasted?"

I said , "Yes."

He said, "Well, I want to tell you an experience we had. We had eight people committed to be baptized,and when we went over to see them, things had occurred that made them where they wouldn't qualify for baptism right now. Probably a little bit later, but not right now. Their baptism would probably have to be postponed a week. You know, President, we were just so committed to having seven or eight baptisms that we decided to do the same things those missionaries did, and we prayed and asked the Lord if He wouldn't bless us to present our message to some that were really prepared to hear it. Then we went to bed."

"Interestingly enough," they said, "At 3:00 a .m. this morning, we received a phone call." (I guess we find the spirit works best at 3:00 a.m. in the morning.) At 3:00 a.m., they received a phone call. A lady on the phone

asked them if they could come over to her house. She said, "We're having some problems and we would like to talk with you."

He didn't remember the name. He didn't know just exactly who it was, but asked the lady how she knew who he was. He had been tracting throughout the area, had gone to their home and they had refused to let him in. He had continued his work, not really thinking too much about it. Later that night, the problems were occurring in this family and they felt a need to have counsel from a minister.

They knew some ministers in the area, but they had felt a good spirit from this young missionary who had come by the door, even though they hadn't let him in. They had remembered his name and in some way were able to find his telephone number. In their hour of need the Lord had somehow directed them to call this missionary. He and his companion went to the home of the family and taught them.

As the Elder talked to me at 6:30 in the morning, he explained, "And you know what, President? There are seven of them that are committed to be baptized this coming Sunday. They're so strong. It seems that we have been able to save their family relationship. Not only that, they have accepted the Gospel, and perhaps we have provided them with some eternal blessings. "

Now here are the things that can happen when you are prepared. When you really love the Lord. Here are some things that say to me, and I'm sure to you, that The

Church of Jesus Christ of Latter-day Saints is the Kingdom of God on earth and that the Lord does honor those who serve Him. Those who fail to recognize the blessings that come with real service, miss out on so much.

CHAPTER NINE

Home to Green Valley Lane

Arrival Home

Coming home from our mission was exciting. Before driving to our home on Green Valley, we drove around town. The Liberty Expressway had been constructed during our absence exactly as I had projected it before leaving on our mission. Several streets and developments had also been constructed the same as I had envisioned prior to leaving. We wondered what it would be like returning to a house with no bed or other furniture. A surprise awaited us.

As we turned the key to unlock our house, there was furniture already located in the first room we entered. Furniture was in the den. Furniture was in our bedroom. Furniture was in almost every room in the house. A good friend, Jan Golden, along with a few other friends, had contacted practically every family that kept our furniture and managed to get most of it moved back into our home before we arrived.

One piece of furniture was missing, our kitchen table. The family that was keeping our kitchen table forgot that it belonged to us and sold it. We never mentioned it to anyone. We were just grateful that most of our furniture was in good condition and back in our home.

While Fonda went about organizing our house, I started back working at Marbury Engineering Company. In just a few days I received a call asking me to meet with the Columbus Georgia stake president, Bill Meadows, at the church building. I was surprised when he asked me to serve as Bishop of the Albany Second Ward. What was even more surprising was that I did not live in that ward. I lived in the boundaries of the Albany First Ward. Regardless, on August 16, 1981, I was sustained as the Bishop of the Albany Second Ward. The ward boundaries were soon changed so that our home was included in the boundaries of the Albany Second Ward.

Restaurant Server Tips Fonda

Times were difficult when we first arrived home. I had no money. I was heavily in debt, and I worked between 50 and 60 hours per week. Nevertheless, Fonda and I went on a date every Friday night. Usually, we went out to eat at Logan's Roadhouse, a restaurant only about one mile from our home. We had one server that we especially liked and always asked for her to be our server each time we went there.

Before long Fonda became great friends with the server. That is the way Fonda is. She just likes everybody, and everybody likes her. Fonda would complement the server on how attentive she was to our needs. Fonda would complement her on her smile, the great service she always gave us, and how neat she always looked. We always ordered the same meal and ofttimes the server would just bring us our meal as soon as we sat down without our even having to order.

After about a year and one half our favorite server told us she was moving and would no longer be able to be our server there at Logan's Roadhouse. We expressed our regrets and told her how we would miss her. As we proceeded to leave her a large tip, she declined the tip. Instead, she rewarded us with a large tip. We tried to refuse, but the server insisted. She told us that we were her favorite customers and no one had ever treated her as nicely as we did, especially Fonda. She said goodbye and gave us both a large hug.

We often hear about how some servers complain that their tips are not large enough. This is the only time I have ever heard of a server tipping the customer.

Scouting in the Church

Fonda and I were returning from a visit to the Atlanta, Georgia Temple of our church on Saturday, June 27, 1987. Our church was having a special meeting that evening and we wanted to be there. A new stake president was to be called. We were curious to know who it would be.

We arrived on time and found two seats near the middle of a row close to the front. As the service proceeded one of the ushers asked me to go into a room to visit with Elder Rex D. Pinegar. Elder Pinegar was a member of the first quorum of seventy and the area president. He would be the one to decide who the next stake president would be.

As we spoke, I told him a man named Clifford Clive would be a wonderful choice. Clifford Clive, however, was out of the state and not available to be interviewed. We spoke for a few minutes more and I returned to my seat.

A short time later I was asked to visit Elder Pinegar again. After another short visit I again returned to my seat. This time the usher requested me to sit at the end of the row so that it would be easier if asked to visit with Elder Pinegar again. Sure enough, for a third time Elder Pinegar wanted to visit with me. He asked Fonda to come with me this time.

On the third visit Elder Pinegar called me to be the stake president of the Columbus Georgia stake. He asked Fonda if she would support me, and of course she said yes. The next day, Sunday, June 28, 1987, I was sustained as the second president of the Columbus Georgia stake of the Church of Jesus Christ of Latter-day Saints. I followed William F Meadows who was the first president of that stake.

Two years later the Church asked Fonda and me to attend scout training at Philmont Scout Ranch in New Mexico. Philmont Scout Ranch is a 140,171-acre ranch among the mountains and mesas of northeastern New Mexico. Elder Von J Featherstone conducted much of the training.

Fonda and I slept in a tent for the entire week's training. Training generally started around 7 AM in the morning, which was much too early for Fonda. Somehow, she always managed to be ready on time since being late meant we would miss the bus that picked us up for scheduled trips. Shc did complain that she needed more time to fix her hair and put on makeup, however. A year later I organized a "Little Philmont" for several stakes in South Georgia.

The Beep Heard Around the Chapel

Fonda played the piano at church for more than fifty years. People loved to hear her play. She had a calm, dignified way about her—exactly the kind of person you want sitting at the organ during a church service.

This was back before cell phones, when we all carried pagers. If someone needed you, they dialed your number and the pager would beep loudly to let you know to find a phone and call them back.

I liked being able to reach Fonda whenever I needed to, so I encouraged her to keep the pager in her purse. She didn't always remember. To solve that problem, I occasionally slipped the pager into her purse without telling her. That way, if I needed her, I knew the pager would be there.

One Sunday, just before church started, I quietly placed the pager in her purse before she sat down at the organ.

The meeting began normally. Fonda played the opening hymn beautifully, as always. When the hymn ended, the congregation bowed their heads for the opening prayer.

Right in the middle of the prayer—

BEEP! Then there were some loud crackling sounds.

The sound echoed through the chapel.

Fonda sat perfectly still for a moment, trying to maintain her usual calm dignity. Then it beeped again.

BEEP! Then more loud crackling sounds followed.

She looked to the left. She looked to the right. She glanced under the bench. The mystery beeping continued, and she had no idea where it was coming from.

All the while, people sat quietly with their heads bowed, pretending not to notice.

From my seat near the front, I knew exactly what was happening. My heart sank. I had forgotten to tell her I'd put the pager in her purse.

Trying not to make things worse than they already were, I stood up, walked to the organ, reached into her purse, and turned off the pager.

Fonda slowly turned and looked at me.

It was one of those looks that clearly said, *"We'll discuss this later."*

The prayer ended, the service continued, and everything went smoothly after that.

When we got home, Fonda didn't say a word. She simply stood there and stared at me.

I stared back.

Then I smiled.

Then I started laughing.

I knew it probably wasn't the best decision, but I didn't know what else to do.

After a moment, Fonda tried to stay serious—but she couldn't help herself. She started laughing too.

That's my wife. Even when I create embarrassing moments, she somehow finds a way to make them pleasant.

The Day Everything Changed

On another occasion Fonda was seated at the organ in our church, playing as the congregation gathered. Music filled the room the way it always did, warm and familiar. But that morning something wasn't right. As she played, she began to feel dizzy.

When the music ended, she stood up from the organ bench and started down the steps toward the congregation. I was sitting near the front of the church, watching as she carefully made her way down. Then I saw her stumble.

Within seconds she was losing her balance and beginning to fall. I jumped to my feet and rushed toward her, nearly knocking one of the ladies in front of me to the floor in my hurry to reach her.

Something was wrong. We both knew it.

Soon afterward I took her to see a doctor. We expected a simple explanation—maybe fatigue, maybe an inner ear problem. But the news we received was far worse than anything we had imagined. The doctor told us Fonda had multiple sclerosis. The words hit us like a blow.

At the time, we had a friend who also suffered from multiple sclerosis, and she could barely walk. Watching her struggle had shown us just how cruel the disease could be. The thought of Fonda slowly losing her ability to walk—or eventually spending the rest of her life in a wheelchair—was almost too much to bear. The diagnosis brought fear, sadness, and a deep sense of uncertainty about the future. But there was one thing I knew immediately: I wasn't going to give up without a fight.

Our local doctors told us there was no cure. They explained that multiple sclerosis was a disease people simply had to learn to live with. That answer didn't sit well with me. I believed there had to be something more that could be done. So I began searching.

I spent countless hours in libraries reading medical journals and books about multiple sclerosis. I combed through research papers, studied treatment programs, and followed every lead I could find. When information began appearing online, I searched the Internet as well.

I was determined to find something—anything—that offered hope. Most of what I discovered was discouraging. Many treatments slowed the disease only slightly, if at all. Few offered meaningful long-term improvement.

Then, during one of my searches, I found a book published on March 24, 1987, by Barbara Dugan titled *The Multiple Sclerosis Diet Book*. The book described a treatment program developed by Dr. Roy Laver Swank based on a low-fat diet. The more I read, the more intrigued I became.

Dr. Swank had spent decades researching the relationship between diet and multiple sclerosis. His long-term studies suggested that patients who followed his strict low-saturated-fat diet often experienced dramatically better outcomes. Many of them either improved slightly or showed little progression of the disease even after ten years.

By comparison, studies from other treatment programs showed far less encouraging results. To me, the conclusion seemed obvious. We needed to see Dr. Swank.

After more searching, I learned that his clinic was located in Portland, Oregon. He operated the Roy Swank Multiple Sclerosis Clinic at Oregon Health & Science University, which was then known as the University of Oregon Medical School.

Getting an appointment was not easy. It took months of persistence and patience, but eventually I was able to schedule a visit. When we finally met Dr. Swank, he confirmed the diagnosis: Fonda did indeed have multiple sclerosis.

He immediately placed her on a strict dietary program. The diet required eliminating processed foods that contain saturated fats or hydrogenated oils. Fonda's daily intake of saturated fat could not exceed fifteen grams. For the first year she was not allowed to eat any red meat, including pork. Skinless poultry and white fish were allowed, but dark poultry meat was discouraged. Dairy products had to contain one percent butterfat or less. Whole-grain breads, rice, and pasta were encouraged, and snacks such as nuts and seeds were recommended as healthy sources of natural oils and energy, as long as they contained little or no saturated fats.

Fonda committed herself fully to the program. She followed the diet faithfully every day. For several years we returned to Portland annually so Dr. Swank could monitor her progress.

I decided that I would follow the diet as well, although I must admit that I wasn't nearly as disciplined as she was. The truth is, aside from the healthy meals Fonda prepared, I often strayed from the diet. Fonda, however, never did.

Today, more than thirty-five years later, the results are remarkable. Fonda still technically has multiple sclerosis, but she shows virtually no symptoms of the disease. She lives a full and active life, something we once feared might never be possible again.

Looking back, we remain deeply grateful for Dr. Swank and the years of research he devoted to understanding this disease.

But most of all, I am grateful for Fonda's determination. Her commitment to that diet, day after day, year after year, gave her the chance to live a normal life. Since her diagnosis in 1990, and now more than thirty-five years later, that decision continues to bless us every single day.

CHAPTER TEN

Disaster Man

Hurricane Andrew

Fonda often called me "disaster man" because of the many natural disasters I helped with. Between the years of 1992 and 2011, it seems I was helping with natural disasters almost every year. The first was Hurricane Andrew.

Although Hurricane Andrew began as a tropical depression. By the time it reached Homestead, Florida, on August 24, 1992, it was a category five hurricane, with sustained wind speeds of 165 mph and gusts as high as 177 mph. It destroyed more than 63,500 houses and damaged more than 124,000 others. It left 65 people dead.

I received a call from church headquarters immediately after Hurricane Andrew touched down in Homestead Florida. I was instructed to organize teams from our church to go to Homestead, Florida and other damaged areas in Florida to help restoration efforts.

Fonda prepared food and lunches to take to Florida

and off we went, several hundred volunteers. Words can't explain what we saw. The City of Homestead, Florida, just didn't seem to exist. It just looked like a flat piece of land. There were no trees standing, no buildings standing, and everything was so destroyed that even the people living there could not find their way around due to the total devastation.

James Sizemore, a member of our church, allowed several of us to go down with him in his motor home to help with the cleanup. Most of us stayed a week spreading tarps over the roof of buildings and helping create tent cities since most of the buildings were totally destroyed. Bill Pitts, another member of our church, stayed much longer to offer additional assistance.

Tropical Storm Alberto

Late 1993 and early 1994 were difficult times for Fonda and me. Fonda's father died September 14, 1993, and my father died February 6, 1994. Shortly afterward, in July, 1994, tropical storm Alberto caused major flooding in Southwest Georgia.

America's, Georgia, received 27 inches of rain with 21 inches falling within 24 hours. Plains, Georgia, got more than 23 inches during that same period. More than 400 coffins from two cemeteries in Albany, Georgia, floated above the ground. Albany State College, which was located along the Flint River, was almost completely submerged as floodwaters peaked above the top of the dam that was constructed to protect the college from floods. Most of downtown Albany was underwater.

A friend of ours sleeping upstairs in the second story of her apartment building on Whispering Pines Road heard running water and got out of bed. There was running water all right. Water was one foot deep on the floor as she stepped out of bed. Luckily, several volunteers in boats paddled up to her apartment and rescued her.

Our home was in one of the highest points in Albany, Georgia, and was therefore not affected by the flood. Mitzi's home was also located in an area not expected to flood, so we were not worried.

We set up the gymnasium in our local church building, which was also on high ground, as a temporary shelter for those affected by the flood. Fonda and I, as well as our daughter, Mitzi, and her husband, Steve, decided to stay in the shelter to assist those needing help. Mitzi and her husband invited a displaced family to stay in their house during the flood.

Soon we received a call from the displaced family.

"Water is rushing down the street. We're getting out of here."

Fonda, Mitzi, Steve and I rushed to Mitzi's home. Water was already inside Mitzi's home and rising. Since the water was only a few inches above the floor, we felt like we could save Mitzi's piano by lifting it off the floor and placing it on her couch. Surely, we thought, the water would not rise another two feet inside her home and damage her piano. We were wrong. However, the rising water only damaged the lower part of the piano. We were able to repair it later.

Fonda was a champion during all of this. She never got flustered. She never considered her own needs, and she constantly did whatever she could to assist those who had to leave their homes because of the flood.

Two years after the Flood of 1994, on August 25, 1996, I was released as stake president.

Valentine's Day Tornado of 2000

Fonda and I were still involved with assisting several flood areas and victims after the flood of 1994. Next came the flood of 1998. Although this flood was not as severe as the flood of 1994, our hometown of Albany, Georgia, sustained significant damage. The flood of 1998 required the evacuation of about 14,000 people.

The Valentine's Day tornado of February 14, 2000, took 19 lives, 11 of which were in Camilla, Georgia, a town just south of our own hometown. Although, to my knowledge, Albany suffered no loss of life, it did suffer considerable damage. Fonda and I spent many days and hours helping with cleanup in the tornado damaged areas, especially in Camilla. It was estimated that as many as 700 houses or mobile homes were damaged or destroyed.

RITCHEY MARBURY HELPING WITH CLEANUP IN VALENTINE'S DAY TORNADO IN CAMILLA GA

Hurricane Katrina

On August 29, 2005, Hurricane Katrina made landfall in Louisiana, resulting in 1,833 fatalities and more than $100 billion worth of damage. Wind speeds reached up to 175 mph and with a storm surge reported to be twenty feet high. More than 15 million people were affected.

Throughout the area looters and robbers tried to take advantage of the difficult conditions in the area. Many homeowners took to defending their home for themselves. The sign in the following picture gives you some idea of what homeowners did to protect their homes and property.

SIGN AT A HOME DURING HURRICANE KATRINA

Shortly after Hurricane Katrina made landfall, Fonda and I drove to Slidell, Louisiana, to help. Fonda was 66 years old, but worked like a 36-year-old.

No one could work as hard as Fonda. She grabbed wheelbarrows, and immediately began removing debris from the property. She spoke to the homeowners and gave them hope just by the positive sound of her voice.

So many people came to help him with recovery support, that I wrote a sonnet about these efforts. I called it "Devastation and Recovery."

FONDA WORKING DURING HURRICANE KATRINA

DEVASTATION AND RECOVERY

So often when we see the devastation
Of hurricanes, tornados, wind and rain,
Of earthquakes and storm surges and the pain
Of millions homeless all throughout the nation,
We wonder if we ever can recover
From loss of power, property and life,
From loss of son and daughter, husband, wife,
And other losses we may soon discover.
But then we see the help come rushing in
From north and south and also east and west,
Both men and women work and do their best
To help us all recover and begin
To know what counts. It's how we'll all endeavor
To share life's tragedies and joys together.

After we returned home, we took a short rest and prepared to go back to Louisiana to help some more. We loaded our car with the necessary provisions and started to leave. The day was September 30, 2005. We didn't make the trip that day.

We heard Fonda's mother coughing in the back of our house. She was struggling to breathe and seemed to be in pain. Quickly we call 911 and the medics arrived shortly after. Even though medics came quickly and did all possible, Fonda's mother died. It was a sad day for us all.

Americus, Georgia Tornado

Early March 2007, a deadly tornado hit Americus, Georgia. Throughout the United States, 57 tornados occurred between February 28 and March 3, 2007. One of them hit Americus, Georgia, an EF-3 tornado, destroying the medical center there. Our family spent much time helping families devastated by the Americus tornado.

Those working at the medical center said it looked like a bomb went off with all the trees down, homes destroyed and power lost. Two people were confirmed dead and many injured due to the tornado. Not only the medical center but also many homes and businesses were completely destroyed.

As soon as it was safe to travel, my family started helping the town. We picked up debris, helped clean yards in damaged homes, and helped distribute supplies that came in from all over the southeast. The Doctor's Pharmacy was destroyed. My wife and I, as well as our daughter, Mitzi, spent days helping with the cleanup.

Albany, Georgia, Tornado of 2017

In 2017 there were more than 1400 confirmed tornados. Our family was heavily involved in the one in our hometown. In January, strong thunderstorms and a tornado hit Albany, Georgia, causing a path of destruction, leaving downed power lines, broken trees and severe structural damage. Again, our family spent many days helping victims.

OUR DAUGHTER, MITZI, HELPING WITH CLEANUP

DESTROYED HOME OF FRIEND—ALBANY 2017 TORNADO

A mobile home park in the east part of town was almost destroyed, as well as homes of our friends. Fonda spent much time preparing meals for families in need while I helped with cleanup.

CHAPTER ELEVEN

Vacations and Special Events

The Anasazi Wilderness Adventure

In 2005, our oldest granddaughter, Katie, was navigating the turbulent waters of extreme anxiety. Seeking a way to support her, Fonda and I—along with Katie's parents, Mitzi and Steve Hunter—turned to a program recommended by our friend, Brent Hosman: the Anasazi Foundation.

Anasazi was a wilderness therapy program that combined clinical management with deep family involvement. The philosophy was simple but profound: strip away the distractions of modern life and let nature teach the soul. In February, we traveled to Mesa, Arizona, to begin the journey. After an orientation, Katie was issued primitive gear—blankets, a canvas pack, and traditional outdoor clothing. She left the modern world behind to hike and camp in the rugged desert, moving to a new spot

KATIE AT ANASAZI

almost every night, far beyond the reach of a phone or the internet.

While Katie was in the wilderness, Fonda and I, and her parents, participated in workshops and weekly coaching sessions. These calls kept us updated on her progress and taught us how to support her journey. The climax of the program came during the final three days, when we traveled into the Arizona backcountry to join Katie on the trail.

To say this was an adventure is an understatement. I was 66 and Fonda was 65; living on the trail was something we never expected to do at our age. We had no matches and had to rely on primitive methods to start a

FONDA WITH HER BACKPACK AT ANASAZI

fire for cooking. Luckily for us, Katie had learned how; she built our fires while I tried—and consistently failed—to do the same.

Never let anyone tell you it doesn't get cold in Arizona. Our trek was marked by biting wind and rain. Thankfully, Katie had also learned to build primitive shelters, which kept us dry. I had arrived shortly before the rest of the family, giving Katie some precious one-on-one time to teach her grandfather the basics of desert survival.

The experience culminated with the entire family—Mitzi, Steve, Katie, Fonda, and I—camping together. We returned home with a profound appreciation for our ancestors and a renewed gratitude for modern conveniences.

KATIE STARTING FIRE WITH NO MATCHES
RITCHEY TRIES TO HELP

RITCHEY AND KATIE AT ANASAZI

RITCHEY AT ANASAZI

PICTURED LEFT TO RIGHT: RITCHEY, FONDA, KATIE, MITZI (KATIE'S MOTHER), STEVE (KATIE'S FATHER)

Walt Disney World: "We're Coming, Mickey!"

If the Arizona desert was our most grueling trip, Walt Disney World was undoubtedly our favorite. We joined the Disney Vacation Club in June 1995 and vacationed there almost every year.

Usually, we made the five-hour drive from Albany, Georgia, in our Chevrolet Suburban. Fonda would sit in the back, fixing sandwiches for us to eat as we rolled south toward Orlando.

Watching the grandchildren was the best part. They would squirm and giggle with glee as we neared the gates. I'll never forget one of the first times we took Katie; she looked up at the entrance sign and shouted at the top of her lungs, "We're coming, Mickey!"

Old Key West Resort was our home away from home. Styled after the fictional "Conch Flats," it felt like a real community with its pastel buildings and palm-lined paths. We usually stayed in a two-bedroom villa with a full kitchen, though we spent most of our time at the parks.

Fonda's favorite attraction was *Soarin' Around the World.* She loved the gentle sensation of hang-gliding over stunning landscapes with the wind and scents of orange groves in the air. Fonda preferred the "slow, calm, and peaceful" side of Disney. Our children and grandchildren, however, had different ideas.

BUILDING SIGN AT DISNEY'S OLD KEY WEST RESORT

Once, they managed to trick Fonda into riding *Space Mountain*. As the coaster plunged into the pitch-black "outer space," Fonda screamed through the entire ride. When we finally off-boarded, she sternly threatened to banish us all into "outer darkness" if we ever tricked her like that again!

We found gentler ways to tease her. Fonda has a lifelong fear of birds, and we once picked an outdoor restaurant where sparrows were known to frequent. A small bird landed near her foot; Fonda flinched and tried to play it cool, but by the end of the meal, we noticed she hadn't eaten a bite. Instead, she had been systematically tossing crumbs into the walkway, creating a "decoy trail" to lure the birds away from her feet. It worked—the sparrows got a feast, and Fonda finally finished her meal in peace.

FONDA AT SUPULPA CITY LIMITS SIGN

A Busy 2007: From Oklahoma to the Nation's Capital

The year 2007 was a whirlwind. We traveled to Sapulpa, Oklahoma—Fonda's birthplace—as well as Washington D.C., and Mount Rushmore.

Our son, Rick, was working in Utah at the time and met us in Sapulpa over Presidents' Day weekend. It was a sentimental journey. We drove out, spent one day exploring, and drove back the next. The highlight was simply watching Fonda smile as she retraced her earliest roots, perhaps for the first time in her memory. We made sure to capture a photo of her standing proudly by the Sapulpa city limits sign.

FONDA AT WELCOME TO SAPULPA SIGN

CHANGING OF THE GUARD

A month later, I was selected as a representative from Georgia to serve on a tax-reduction committee in Washington D.C. We succeeded in doing so, but the trip was memorable for much more than politics. We visited the Lincoln Memorial, the White House, and watched the Changing of the Guard at Arlington National Cemetery.

We also visited the Uncle Remus Museum in Eatonton, Georgia, with Katie. The museum honors Joel Chandler Harris, whose stories of Br'er Rabbit and Br'er Fox delighted generations. It was a fun experience to a busy year.

KATIE AT UNCLE REMUS MUSEUM

RITCHEY AND FONDA AT UNCLE REMUS MUSEUM

Fun in Nauvoo

Fonda and I often visited Nauvoo and surrounding areas. The Nauvoo pageant and British pageant told stories of early Latter-day Saints in Illinois and the British Isles. Although we very much enjoyed these two pageants, often we enjoyed the program, "Sunset on the Mississippi," even more. Admission was free and the cast consists of talented young missionaries performing a diverse range of acts, music, and entertainment.

When we first visited Nauvoo, "Sunset on the Mississippi" was performed on the banks of the Mississippi River. Later it was performed on an outdoor stage a few blocks from the Mississippi River.

Fonda always had a special brand of motherly pride. She would often joke that our son, Rick, was so outstanding he could "walk on water." During one winter visit, Rick decided to give her a "miracle." The Mississippi River had frozen solid, and Rick walked out about fifty feet onto

RICK "WALKS ON WATER"

the ice. Fonda didn't skip a beat. She just smiled at me and said, "See? I told you our son could walk on water."

The 50th Anniversary: From Florida to the Last Frontier

June 16, 2012, marked fifty married years of "love, life, and laughter." To celebrate, we planned a massive tour of the United States, stretching from the tip of Florida all the way to Anchorage, Alaska. After this trip was completed, Fonda and I had visited all 50 states together.

Our anniversary began with a delicious meal prepared by Stonebridge Country Club. We had all planned to eat at the club, but Rick arrived in late afternoon so we could not do that. Mitzi, however, went to Stonebridge, ordered and picked up a meal consisting of sirloin steak, baked potatoes, cucumbers, a salad, and other delicacies. The next day we left for our adventure. Mitzi stayed home, but Rick went on the anniversary trip with us.

Rick took the wheel for most of the trek through the Midwest, while Fonda and I sat in the back, holding hands and watching the Great Lakes and the plains of the Dakotas roll by.

After driving many miles, Rick decided to stop and take a nap. He chose to stop in Wahpeton North Dakota.

We stopped to see "Geese in Flight"—a massive metal sculpture in North Dakota—and visited Old Faithful in Yellowstone before flying from Utah to Alaska.

OUR FAMILY–LEFT TO RIGHT: KATIE (GRANDDAUGHTER), MITZI (DAUGHTER), RICK (SON), KIM (GRANDDAUGHTER), AND KERI (GRANDDAUGHTER)

RICK NAPPING AT WAHPETON

FONDA AND RITCHEY AT “GEESE IN FLIGHT”

OLD FAITHFUL AT YELOWSTONE PARK

RITCHEY AND FONDA IN 2-SEATER UTV

Alaska was a revelation. Being used to the rhythm of the Georgia sun, the "Midnight Sun" threw us for a loop—it was still broad daylight at midnight! Instead of renting a car, we took a train into the mountains and then rented a two-seater UTV (Utility Task Vehicle).

I wasn't sure if Fonda would go for the rugged off-road bouncing, but she was a trooper. There we were—helmets on, cold wind biting our cheeks, navigating the Alaskan wilderness side-by-side. It proved that no matter our age, we were still up for an adventure. It was a joy to also have Rick with us.

Buying a ticket on the Glacier Express, we cruised through Prince William Sound to watch the ice on Blackstone Glacier slide into the sea. Seeing that ancient ice

RICK, FONDA, AND RITCHEY IN ALASKA

RICK, FONDA AND RITCHEY ON GLACIER EXPRESS

FONDA AND RITCHEY AT BLACKSTONE GLACIER

slide into the water was a powerful reminder: while the world is always shifting, our love remains as solid as the mountains.

FONDA PETS SLED DOG AT JEFF KING'S HUSKY HOMESTEAD

Before leaving, we visited Jeff King's Husky Homestead near Denali to see the sled dogs. Although they weren't supposed to be petted, one husky rushed straight for Fonda. It seems even Alaskan sled dogs couldn't resist her spirit.

Our final thrill was a bus ride through Denali National Park, where we saw a grizzly bear chasing a hiker! Luckily, the hiker was rescued by a bus behind us. Fonda and I decided right then and there that we would never hike or camp in Denali National Park.

We finished the journey with some King Salmon fishing. While Fonda stayed at the hotel, Rick and I hit the water. We weren't allowed to keep the fish we caught due to current regulations, but we had fun just catching the fish.

It was a tiring trip, but as we returned home, we felt immensely blessed. Fifty years was just the beginning; there were many more years of love, life, and laughter yet to come.

FONDA AND RITCHEY BOARD BUS AT DENALI NATIONAL PARK

GRIZZLY BEAR THAT CHASED HIKER

RICK FISHES FOR KING SALMON

RICK CATCHES KING SALMON

CHAPTER TWELVE

The Years Roll On

Home Gardens

The years have a quiet way of moving forward. At the time, each day seemed ordinary—planting a garden, visiting family, fixing things around the house. But when you look back, those ordinary days are what make up a life. For Fonda and me, many of those memories were tied to our home and the routines we shared together.

For many years Fonda and I planted a garden, and it seemed to grow a little larger every year. Our first garden was only twenty feet by twenty feet. It was small, but it produced enough vegetables to make us glad.

The next year we expanded it to twenty by forty feet. Then it grew again to twenty by sixty. Before long we were tending a garden twenty feet by eighty feet across the back yard.

What had started as a simple backyard project slowly turned into a serious garden. And it produced beautifully.

We grew corn, cantaloupes, string beans, radishes, onions, and sometimes watermelons. There is something especially satisfying about eating food that comes directly from your own soil. Every harvest reminded us that the effort had been worth it.

Of course, there was one problem. Keeping the weeds under control.

I was very good at preparing the soil and planning what we would plant each year. I enjoyed the beginning of the season when the rows were straight, and everything looked neat and promising.

But I was not nearly as good at the constant work of weeding. Sometimes the weeds grew so tall that Fonda had trouble finding the vegetables she had come out to pick. The neighbors occasionally joked with her, warning that if she wasn't careful, she might reach down and pick up a snake hiding in the tall weeds. We laughed about it, but there was some truth to it.

Looking back, those gardens were not just about vegetables. They were part of the rhythm of our lives—something we worked on together year after year.

As time passed and we grew older, bending over rows of plants became more difficult. Planting and harvesting crops that grew close to the ground took more effort than it once had. So, we decided to build a raised garden bed.

We stacked concrete blocks to create a long bed about a foot and a half high, three feet wide, and roughly forty feet long. It wasn't fancy, but it worked perfectly.

FONDA, MITZI, AND RICK CONSTRUCTING A RAISED GARDEN

RAISED GARDEN READY TO HARVEST

Rick and Mitzi helped us get it ready, and we had a local company bring in fresh soil to fill it. After that, planting and harvesting became much easier.

The garden thrived. Corn grew at one end, and lettuce, radishes, and onions filled the other. Fonda planted tomatoes in a grow box near the side of the house.

Even today, when I think about those gardens, I remember not only the vegetables but the time we spent working side by side.

Fonda's Sister Dies

In early 2015 we received troubling news. Fonda's sister, Carol Ann Creech, was in poor health. We decided to travel to Cleveland, Tennessee, to visit her. Looking back now, we were very thankful that we made that trip.

On August 12, 2015, Carol passed from this life to the next. She had been well known and loved throughout the City of Cleveland. Her kindness had touched many people, and it was clear from the large number who attended her funeral. Carol died from cancer, and her passing left a deep sadness among family and friends.

At the reception afterward, several people looked closely at Fonda and commented on how much she resembled her sister. Some even had to take a second look.

Fonda accepted that as a compliment. In a small way, it felt like a reminder that part of her sister still lived on.

Not long after Carol passed away, her husband Bill Creech also died. Losing them both so close together was painful for everyone who knew them. But they had lived a full life together—traveling to many cities and countries and enjoying their years to the fullest. Sometimes the best comfort is remembering that a person truly lived.

Mission Reunion

In early January 2016, I spoke with several former missionaries who had served while I was mission president about the idea of holding a mission reunion. It had been

35 years since I was released, and many of them felt it would be wonderful to see each other again and remember those special years we had shared. When I mentioned the idea to Fonda, she immediately loved it, and together we began making plans.

Rick was living in Utah at the time, so we asked him where he thought would be a good place to hold the reunion. He suggested the BYU Wilkinson Student Center, which sounded perfect. We decided on Friday, September 30, 2016, as the date. That timing worked especially well because it was the day before the Church's general conference, when many people would already be traveling to Utah.

When the day finally arrived, it turned out to be a wonderful and memorable event. Many of our former missionaries came, and it was a joy to see them again after so many years. Some had changed very little, while others were almost unrecognizable at first, but the bond we shared quickly brought back the memories of those days in the mission field.

Throughout the evening we shared stories about our missionary experiences. Some stories filled the room with laughter, while others reminded us of the powerful spiritual moments we had experienced together.

One of the most amusing stories came from a missionary who reminded us that he had actually won a horse while serving his mission. Somehow, he arranged for friends in Idaho to care for the horse until his mission was finished. When he returned home, he went back to Idaho, picked up the horse, and took it home with him. It was the kind of story that no one would believe unless they had heard it from the missionary himself.

Other missionaries shared meaningful experiences about people they had taught and baptized, and the ways the Lord had blessed them during their service. As I listened to these stories, I was reminded that the mission had not only changed the lives of the people we taught, but also the lives of the missionaries who served there.

That evening was more than just a reunion. It was a reminder of the faith, sacrifice, and dedication of those young missionaries so many years earlier. Seeing them again as husbands, fathers, and leaders in their communities was deeply rewarding. It reaffirmed to me that the influence of missionary service lasts a lifetime and that the blessings from those years continue long after the mission itself has ended.

Fonda Breaks Her Hip

On November 25, 2017, Fonda decided the carpets needed cleaning. Personally, I thought they looked fine. But once Fonda decided something needed to be done, it was usually going to get done. She scheduled a carpet cleaning service to come to the house.

Of course, before allowing anyone else to clean the house, Fonda wanted the house cleaned first. That was simply her way of doing things. By the time the cleaners arrived, she had already been busy working around the house.

While they cleaned the carpets, they also washed the kitchen floor. When they finished, the floor was extremely slick. Fonda was still moving quickly from room to room, continuing her own cleaning, when suddenly she slipped and fell.

I hurried to her side and asked what had happened. Without hesitation she answered, "I've fallen and I can't get up."

It sounded exactly like the line from the well-known television commercial, and even in that moment it caught my attention. But the situation was serious.

I rushed her to the emergency room at Phoebe Putney Hospital. The receptionist recognized her and immediately had her taken in to see a doctor. The doctor also knew her and quickly evaluated the injury. Within minutes she was scheduled for surgery with one of the best orthopedic surgeons in the city.

The operation went well. The surgeon repaired her hip, and Fonda remained in the hospital for rehabilitation and physical therapy. We had planned to travel to Utah that Christmas to spend the holidays with our children, Mitzi and Rick. Those plans obviously had to change.

Rick flew down on December 12 to greet Fonda when she got out of the hospital on December 13. He then flew back on the nineteenth.

Mitzi flew down December 20 to visit Fonda, and then flew back a day or two later to take Katie to Kim and

Caleb's wedding. Kim, our youngest granddaughter, was marrying Caleb Conners on December 26, 2017.

Mitzi and Katie flew back to Albany on December 28, and Mitzi stayed with us until after New Year's Day, flying back on January 2, 2018. Fonda and I spent Christmas alone that Christmas.

While Fonda was in the hospital, each day included several sessions of physical therapy followed by time resting in her hospital bed. One thing about Fonda never changed. Even in the hospital, she still managed to enjoy her sweet snacks whenever she could.

In many ways, that small detail captured something important about her—no matter what life brought, she always found a way to enjoy the little things.

Ritchey Breaks His Hip

Fonda recovered quickly from her broken hip and soon returned to her usual routine, energetically managing our home. Around that same time, I heard about the Georgia Golden Olympics table tennis tournament. My friend William O. Herrington and I often played table tennis together, and we decided to enter the competition. William liked to call himself "WOH"—his initials—because he thought it sounded like an interesting nickname.

The tournament was scheduled for September 28, 2018, in the McIntyre Room of the Warner Robins Recreation Department. The winners would be recognized as the Georgia Golden Olympics state champions in table

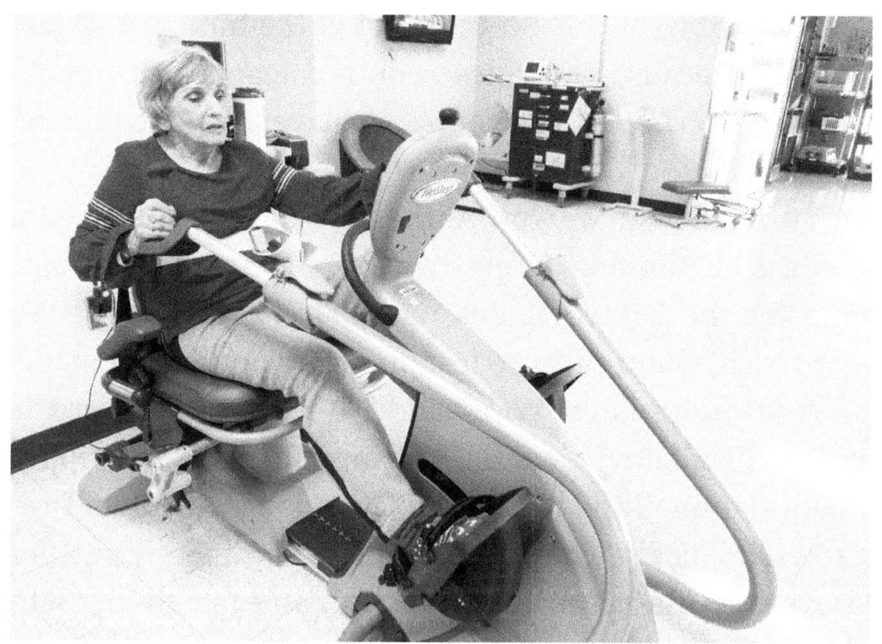

FONDA ON PHYSICAL THERAPY MACHINE

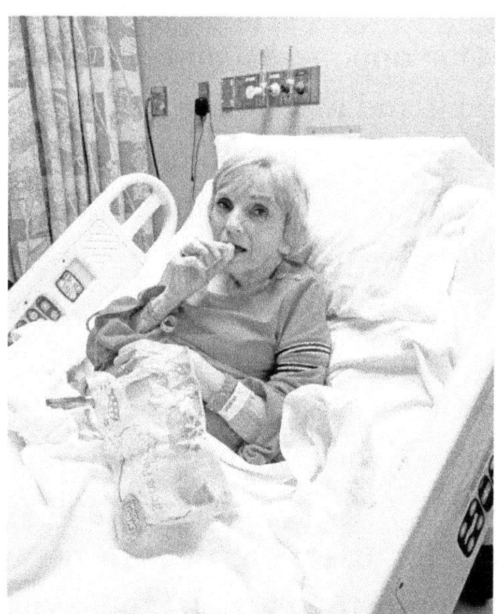

FONDA IN HOSPITAL EATING CANDY

tennis doubles. I was 80 years old at the time, and WOH was 56. Because the rules required teams to compete in the age group of the youngest player, we entered the 55–60 division.

To our delight, we won. As the Georgia state gold-medal doubles champions in our division, we qualified to compete for the United States national championship. We were excited and eager to test ourselves on a bigger stage.

A few days later, WOH and I were practicing at the YMCA in Albany, Georgia. During one rally, our opponents slammed the ball to the left side of the table. I returned it quickly. They sent it back safely, and my partner drove it across again. The next shot came fast to the right side of the table. It was my turn.

I hurried across the floor and managed a careful return. Unfortunately, I slipped as I did so and crashed to the floor. Our opponents sent the ball back, but my partner missed it and we lost the point.

I tried to stand up—but couldn't. YMCA staff quickly called an ambulance. At the hospital, an X-ray confirmed the problem: I had broken my hip.

I called Fonda to tell her the news. She was sympathetic, but she couldn't resist teasing me. She said I had probably broken my hip just to receive the same sympathy she had gotten when she broke hers.

WOH had his own reaction. He joked that he was angry with me for breaking my hip because it ruined our chance to compete for the national championship. I reminded him that I had broken my hip trying to win the point—and that he was the one who missed the return.

During my surgery and physical therapy, Fonda stayed with me most of the time, offering steady support. Even so, she never let me forget her theory that I had broken my hip mainly to compete with her for sympathy.

Christmas 2018

Christmas of 2018 remains my favorite Christmas. The reason is simple, though the meaning has grown deeper with time. It was the last Christmas that Fonda and I were able to spend with all of our children and grandchildren together. At the time, none of us fully understood how precious that gathering would be, but somehow, I felt it.

I was still recovering from a broken hip that year. Moving around was slow and painful, and traveling was not easy. Still, I was determined that nothing would keep me from spending Christmas with my family.

Just a few days before Christmas, Fonda and I boarded a plane in Albany, Georgia. From there we flew to Atlanta, and then continued on to Salt Lake City, Utah. I remember sitting on the plane beside Fonda, both of us a little tired from the effort of travel but happy to be on our way. Family has a way of giving you strength you didn't know you had.

When we arrived in Salt Lake City, our son Rick was there waiting for us at the airport. Seeing him standing there brought an immediate feeling of comfort. He helped us gather our things and drove us to his home in Herriman. At that time our daughter Mitzi was living there with him, which made the house feel even more like the center of our family.

It was already a busy and joyful time for everyone. Our middle granddaughter, Keri, was graduating from BYU Idaho, and Fonda and I had carefully planned our trip so we could attend the ceremony. We were proud of her and looked forward to sharing that important moment in her life. But life has a way of interrupting even the best plans.

Shortly after we arrived, I discovered that I had developed a hernia that required surgery. It grew more intense, and there was no putting it off. Arrangements were made for me to have the operation there in Utah. Because of that, I was unable to attend Keri's graduation.

Fonda had every reason to go to the ceremony and celebrate with the rest of the family, but she refused to leave my side. She stayed with me through the entire ordeal. That was Fonda—steady, loyal, and loving. She believed that being together mattered more than anything else.

Modern medicine still amazes me when I think back on it. I went into the hospital that morning, had surgery later that same day, and by that evening I was back at Rick's home. I was sore and moving very slowly, but I was grateful just to be there.

When we arrived at the house, I faced another small challenge. The pain made it difficult for me to climb the stairs getting inside the house. Rick, however, had already been thinking ahead. Knowing my condition, he had installed sturdy handrails on both sides of the steps so I would have something to hold on to.

With those rails I carefully made my way up the steps and into the house. It may not sound like much, but at that moment it felt like a small victory. Once inside, I settled into a chair and simply watched for a while, taking it all in. Christmas came a few days later.

That was when it truly sank in. Everyone was there. Fonda, my wife; Mitzi and Rick, my children; Katie, Keri, and Kim, my grandchildren; and Kim's new husband, Caleb Connors, who had recently joined our family. The house was full, just the way home should be at Christmas.

At the time, the others may have simply seen it as another family Christmas—busy, noisy, and happy. But for me, it felt different. I sensed how special the moment was, even if I could not fully explain why.

Looking back now, I understand it clearly. That Christmas of 2018 was the last time that Fonda and I would ever spend Christmas together with our daughter Mitzi. And that is why it will always remain my favorite Christmas.

Fonda Has a Mild Stroke

Shortly after we returned home from our Christmas visit with our children, Fonda had a routine dental appointment. Early that morning I left for work in Cordele, Georgia. Before I walked out the door, she fixed me a simple breakfast—orange juice and a peanut butter sandwich. It was an ordinary morning, and neither of us had any reason to think the day would turn out any differently.

Since the dental appointment seemed routine, I drove on to Cordele while Fonda headed to the dentist. About midmorning, my phone rang at the office. It was the dentist's office.

They told me Fonda had suddenly become very dizzy and could barely walk. They had called 911. An ambulance had arrived and taken her to the emergency room at Phoebe Putney Hospital in Albany, Georgia. I left my office immediately.

I'm sure the police were generous with me that day. The drive from Cordele to Albany is about forty miles, but I made it in a little over thirty minutes.

When I rushed into the hospital's emergency room, they would not let me go in. I had to wait outside while the doctors examined her. Those minutes felt much longer than they probably were.

Finally, the doctor came out and spoke to me. He said Fonda had suffered a mild stroke. She stayed overnight in the hospital and came home the next day. When I asked how she felt, she simply said she was fine and planned to go right on doing whatever she wanted.

That was Fonda. I could never tell whether she was feeling good or bad because she always kept the same positive attitude. No matter what was going on, she would smile and say she was fine. Still, I wasn't so sure.

Within a week of the stroke, she was right back to her

normal routine—cooking meals, cleaning the house, and going shopping.

I told her that if she went shopping, she couldn't spend more than five dollars. She just smiled at me, reminded me she had a credit card, and bought whatever she wanted anyway. I must admit, though, Fonda was always a careful and thrifty shopper. She never spent more than she really needed to.

Mitzi Leaves This Life

November 2019 began like any other ordinary month. Fonda and I rose around 5:45 a.m. I took a shower while she prepared breakfast and packed a lunch for me to take on my way to work in Cordele, Georgia. At 6:30 a.m., I left the house and drove to Cordele, arriving around 7:30 that morning. Nothing about the morning seemed unusual.

Later that morning, while I was sitting at my desk in the office, the phone rang. It was Rick. Within moments, his words changed everything. Mitzi's cancer was getting worse.

She had been diagnosed with stage four cancer some time earlier, but we had believed she was improving. The doctors had recommended chemotherapy, but Mitzi chose instead to pursue natural treatments. She did not want to endure the difficult side effects that chemotherapy often brings. Now Rick told us the doctor had said she likely had only a few weeks to live.

When I heard those words, I knew we needed to go to

Utah immediately. I told the office in Cordele that Fonda and I would be leaving right away. Everyone there was understanding and assured me they would be praying for our daughter. The next day we boarded a plane and traveled to Utah.

During those final weeks, we were deeply touched by the many friends who came to visit and comfort Mitzi. Their kindness meant more to us than words can express. Kathy Loman Blocker came almost every day, bringing candy and small gifts to brighten Mitzi's day. Kathy and Mitzi had been close friends since Mitzi's childhood, and their bond remained strong.

Mitzi also had a special group of friends who called themselves "The Three Mitzi's." They came often to visit as well. Friends from Mitzi's church in Herriman, Utah, along with friends who had moved to Utah from Albany, Georgia, came to spend time with her and offer their love and support.

Our son Rick was remarkable during that time. He cared for Mitzi constantly—bringing her food, taking her to doctor appointments, and making sure she was as comfortable as possible. He even arranged for a television in her room that she could easily control with a remote.

Just before she passed away, I was able to spend a little quiet time alone with Mitzi. I sat beside her bed and held her hand. We didn't talk very much. Words were not necessary. In that quiet moment, we both felt the deep love we had always shared.

Mitzi left this life in the early morning hours of Saturday, November 30, 2019, just 22 months after she was diagnosed with breast cancer.

The last thing Fonda said to her was, "I love you, Mitzi."

Mitzi's final words were, "I love you too."

Her funeral was held at 11:00 a.m. on Tuesday, December 3, 2019, at the Herriman Rose First Ward building. Edgar Cheney, a member of the ward bishopric, spoke, along with our close friend Bob Oates. Mitzi was laid to rest at the Herriman City Cemetery, and I had the sacred privilege of dedicating her grave.

Fonda and I felt great comfort from the many friends who came to the funeral. When we looked around the chapel and saw it filled with people who loved Mitzi, it brought us peace. Some had traveled from far away, and we were not even sure how everyone had learned about it on such short notice. The staff from my City of Cordele office even sent beautiful flowers for the service, a gesture that meant a great deal to us.

CHAPTER THIRTEEN

We Move to Utah

Leaving Green Valley

Our home at 1824 Green Valley Lane in Albany, Georgia, was meant to be our forever home. It was the home we had dreamed about and planned carefully over the years. I had designed the subdivision myself, and Fonda had convinced me to lower the street by four feet so she could live on a hill. The lot was nearly an acre, and it felt like the perfect place to spend the rest of our lives.

When we first built the house, it was only 1,800 square feet. Over the years, as our lives grew and changed, the house grew with us until it reached 4,000 square feet. It had four bedrooms, five bathrooms, and a large 400-square-foot office that could easily serve as another bedroom.

The backyard held three storage sheds, a large raised garden, and a spacious screened-in porch where we often sat in the evenings. We knew nearly everyone on the street, and many of our neighbors had become close friends. We shared time together, along with vegetables from our gardens.

There was no better location in the city. Our street had almost no traffic except for the few families who lived there. It curved gently and stretched only one block long, making it feel private and peaceful.

Golf had long been one of my favorite pastimes, and I was fortunate to have complimentary memberships at two golf clubs, both less than five minutes from our home. Many Friday evenings, Fonda and I would go out for dinner at one of the club restaurants, enjoying the quiet rhythm of a life we had built together. Everything we needed was close by. Our church was only a mile away. Shopping was a mile away. Even our doctor's office was just a mile from the house.

Albany was more than simply the place we lived. It was part of our family's history. Many of the streets and subdivisions throughout the city and surrounding areas had been designed by my grandfather, my father, myself, or my son. Our family's work had helped shape the community.

Albany was where Fonda and I met, and the home on Green Valley Lane was where we spent most of our life together. In many ways, it felt like the center of our world. But life has a way of changing plans.

Our daughter was buried in Utah. Our son Rick lived there as well, along with our youngest granddaughter and great-grandson. Fonda and I were both in our eighties, and Rick was living alone. As much as we loved Albany, the pull of family grew stronger each year. Finally, we knew it was time to move.

We set our moving date for July 21, 2021, and I gave the City of Cordele six months' notice that we would be leaving. Those six months were some of the hardest we had experienced in a long time. We sorted through decades of memories—furniture, books, photographs, and keepsakes. We gave some things away, but many items carried too many memories to part with.

The goodbyes were just as difficult. The City of Cordele held a farewell gathering for us. Our church hosted another, and Lanier Engineering gave us a warm send-off as well. Fonda and I had worked closely with many of the people in those organizations over the years, and the staff at Lanier Engineering included many friends and former colleagues.

Each goodbye reminded us how deeply rooted our lives had become in that community. The move was bittersweet. We were happy knowing we would soon be close to our family, but leaving our home—and the life we had built there—was painful. Fonda cried.

Rick flew down from Utah to meet us and drive us back. We hired movers to pack and transport our furniture. Larry Walden, a close friend and president of Walden and Kirkland Realtors, handled the sale of our home.

My cousin, Suzann Hagins, helped us pack during those final days. When everything was finally ready, she stood outside and waved goodbye as we pulled away.

As we drove down Green Valley Lane for the last time,

we were leaving behind far more than a house. We were leaving behind a lifetime. And ahead of us, a new chapter in Utah was about to begin.

Our 60th Wedding Anniversary

June 16, 2022, was a day that Fonda and I had been looking forward to for a long time. Sixty years of love, life, and laughter together as husband and wife was a remarkable milestone, and we felt it deserved a special celebration.

Just as Rick had done for our mission reunion, he reserved the BYU Wilkinson Student Center for our anniversary celebration. It was the perfect place to gather family and friends and reflect on the many blessings we had experienced during our sixty years of marriage together.

It had been just under a year since we moved from our longtime home in Georgia to our new home in Herriman, Utah. The move had been a big change for us, but we were finally settling in and becoming comfortable in our new surroundings. One of the main reasons for the move was to be closer to our family, and this celebration felt like a wonderful way to bring everyone together.

We sent invitations far and wide—to family and friends from Georgia, and to missionaries who had served with us in the Idaho Pocatello and Idaho Boise missions. In the invitations, we reminded everyone that we had moved from Albany, Georgia, to Herriman, Utah, in July 2021 so we could be nearer to our loved ones.

The evening turned out to be everything we had hoped for. Friends reunited, stories were shared, and laughter filled the room. It was a joyful reminder of the many relationships and memories that had blessed our lives over the years.

The celebration was a great success. Everyone had a wonderful time—but none more than Fonda and me.

Albany Ward 50th Anniversary Celebration

Some anniversaries pass quietly. Others bring the past rushing back in a way that reminds you how deeply people and places have shaped your life.

It seemed that our first few years in Utah were filled with anniversary celebrations. One year after we moved there, Fonda and I celebrated our 60th wedding anniversary. Then, not long afterward, another milestone arrived—the 50th anniversary of the Albany Ward.

The Tallahassee Florida Stake of The Church of Jesus Christ of Latter-day Saints was organized on January 21, 1973. On that same day, the Albany, Georgia Ward was created. I had been serving as president of the Albany Branch and was the last to hold that position before the branch became a ward. Clifford Clive was called as the first bishop of the newly organized Albany Ward, and Fonda, of course, continued faithfully serving as the organist.

As the 50th anniversary approached, several members of the original Albany Ward were now living in Utah.

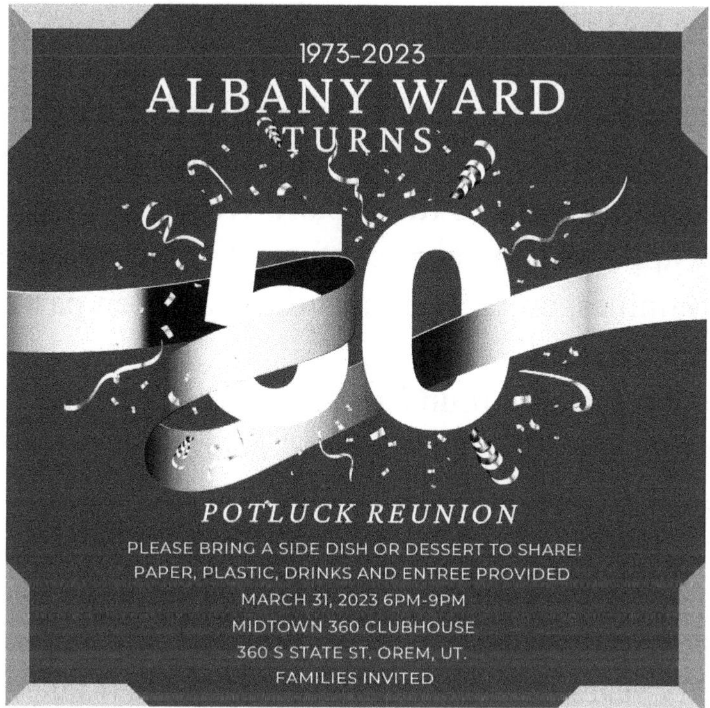

Someone suggested that we should gather and celebrate that special milestone together.

Much of the credit for organizing the event goes to Mindy Oates Sumsion. Before her marriage she was known as Mindy Oates, and her family had been among the original members of the Church in Albany, Georgia. She arranged for the reunion to be held at a clubhouse in Orem, Utah, where her sister Michelle lived.

We were amazed at how many people attended and at the distances some had traveled to be there. Since Fonda and I had only recently moved from Albany, we were probably the only ones present who knew everyone in attendance. For us, it was especially meaningful to greet friends we had seen only recently as well as those we had not seen for nearly fifty years.

The evening included a potluck dinner, and a slide-show was projected on a screen showing photographs from earlier years in the Albany Ward. As image after image appeared, memories returned—of meetings, activities, families, and friendships that had been part of our lives for decades.

As we looked around the room that evening, it was clear that the Albany Ward had been more than just a place where we attended church. It had been a place where lifelong friendships were formed, where families grew, and where many of the most meaningful chapters of our lives unfolded.

Fifty years had passed, and our lives had taken us in many different directions. Yet for one evening in Utah, it felt as though time had gently folded back on itself, and we were once again a ward family gathered together.

Beau

Fonda has always loved animals with a level of devotion usually reserved for grandchildren, heirlooms, and really good desserts. Back in Albany, Georgia, our home always had something furry or slightly mischievous living in it. There was noise, movement, and just enough chaos to make life interesting.

Then we moved to Utah. Suddenly, the house was quiet. Too quiet. Suspiciously quiet. Nothing barked, scratched at the door, or stared at us while we ate dinner. At first, you might think that sounds peaceful. It is not. It is unsettling.

Fonda felt it most. The house didn't just feel empty—it felt like it was missing something. What she wanted—what she was absolutely determined to have—was a small dog.

Our friends, David and Charlee Hanna, pointed us in the right direction. They told us about Ganene Taylor, who runs Paw Place Breeding in Salem, Utah. She raised Cavapoos—a mix of a Cavalier King Charles Spaniel and a Poodle. In other words, a breed specifically designed to be adorable, affectionate, and completely incapable of being ignored. Rick made the arrangements, and on Saturday, August 10, 2024, we went to see them.

The moment we stepped inside Ganene's home, we were greeted by what can only be described as a full-scale Cavapoo welcoming committee. It was a cheerful, bouncing, tail-wagging swarm. If we had stood still long enough, we might have been adopted ourselves.

Ganene welcomed us warmly and led us into her den. She then brought in several Cavapoos waiting to be admired. One particular puppy had already taken matters into his own paws.

Fonda spotted him and he seemed to have spotted her. In that instant, he made his move. He waddled, crawled around, and practically declared himself hers. He was tiny, soft, and equipped with just a few white spots on his foot and head—as if someone had added a little extra charm for emphasis. He and Fonda seemed to have chosen each other. And that was the end of any serious discussion.

His father was a toy poodle named Boomer, and his mother was a Cavalier King Charles Spaniel named Millie. He was just under a month old, born on July 22, 2024—small enough to fit in your hands, but already fully capable of taking over your heart. We made arrangements right then and there. Resistance was not an option.

The next challenge was naming him. We considered several names and our oldest granddaughter, Katie, suggested "Beau." That was the name of a famous southern general, General Beauregard. That name was kind of like calling him, General Beau, a name that outranks his size. We all agreed. Beau it was.

We brought him home on Fonda's birthday, September 12, 2024. From the moment he crossed the threshold, Beau transformed the house. The silence disappeared. In its place came tiny footsteps, playful energy, and the occasional "What has he got now?" moment.

Shoes were no longer safe. Neither were socks. Or anything that looked remotely chewable, movable, or interesting—which, as it turns out, is everything. But along with the mischief came something better. Warmth.

Beau didn't just live in the house—he filled it. He followed us from room to room, as if conducting important inspections. He greeted everyone like they were long-lost family. And he had a way of looking at you that made you feel like you were the most important person in the

BEAU

world—even if he had looked at someone else the exact same way just seconds earlier.

The whole family fell in love with him, but Beau made one thing very clear. Fonda was his person. Where she went, he went. If she sat down, he was beside her or in her lap. If she stood up, he was ready. If she left the room, he followed as if his entire purpose in life depended on keeping her in sight. And maybe it did.

Fonda had wanted a small dog. What she got was a constant companion, a source of laughter, a little bit of trouble, and a whole lot of love wrapped up in fur and personality. And somehow, in the way only a small dog can manage, Beau didn't just fill the house, he filled a space we hadn't quite been able to name. And once he did, we couldn't imagine life without him.

Grateful for Doctors

Looking back, it seems we moved to Utah at exactly the right time. Sometimes Fonda and I joke that we must be part of the doctors' retirement plan, because soon after arriving we began visiting them regularly. It seemed that almost every month either she or I had another appointment.

Most of those visits in 2021 were routine. But beginning in 2022, things started to become more serious. After one routine checkup, my doctor suggested I be tested for cancer. On June 9, 2022, I met with Dr. L. Scott Chidester. The tests confirmed that I had bladder cancer, and surgery was scheduled for June 22.

Five days after the surgery, I returned to see Dr. Chidester. During that visit he explained that the cancer was very aggressive. Because of that, I underwent a second surgery on August 17.

Further tests showed that the cancer was continuing to return, so Dr. Chidester prescribed weekly BCG treatments. To be honest, I never really understood what BCG stood for, but I created my own meaning for it: "Bladder Cancer Go-away."

Between October 6 and December 7, 2022, I received

seven BCG treatments. Unfortunately, on Friday the 13th in January 2023, I learned the cancer had returned again. I'm not superstitious, but I have to admit it was an interesting day to receive that news.

On January 18, 2023, I had my third bladder cancer surgery. Afterward, Dr. Chidester scheduled another round of BCG treatments, which I received between March 8 and April 12.

Through all of this, Fonda and our son Rick were wonderful. They were with me at every surgery and every treatment. The BCG treatments usually made me feel weak and sick for the first three days afterward. Still, I tried to keep things in perspective. I would remind everyone that I only felt bad three days out of the week and felt good the other four. That meant I felt good most of the week.

Then something happened that none of us expected. On the evening of April 27, 2023, Fonda walked into our bedroom stumbling. She looked confused and completely disoriented. When I tried to talk with her, she barely understood what I was saying. I immediately called Rick and told him we needed to get her to the emergency room. Something was terribly wrong.

Rick arrived right away, and we rushed her to Riverton Hospital. Dr. Adam F. Gibbs examined her and ran several tests. The diagnosis was a small stroke caused by extremely high blood pressure. She was treated with medication and monitored for a while before being released to return home.

But in the middle of all that, what was Fonda worried about? Earlier that afternoon a friend, Michelle Oates, had come by to give her a haircut and beauty treatment. Fonda's biggest concern during the hospital visit was that it might mess up her hair. That was Fonda.

Only a week later, on May 5, Rick and I had to rush her to the emergency room again. A normal blood pressure reading is about 120/80. When we arrived, her blood pressure was 181/95. By ten o'clock that evening it had climbed to 239/124.

Thankfully, Dr. Nathan M. Finnerty was the attending physician that night. He prescribed a new medication that worked well. Since then, Fonda has stayed on that medication and her blood pressure has remained mostly within a normal range. But May wasn't finished with us yet.

On May 28, we went to visit a dear friend from Albany, Georgia, Ann Holloman. She was in her nineties and was visiting her son in Utah for her birthday. As Fonda stepped into the house, she tripped and fell hard onto the floor. She was in a great deal of pain, so we called an ambulance.

Although we were in Provo, we asked the ambulance crew if they could take her to Riverton Hospital instead. Fortunately, they agreed.

The next day—Memorial Day, May 29—Fonda underwent surgery performed by Dr. Peterson. The fall had broken her right arm, her right hip, and one right rib. She spent several weeks in the hospital and was then transferred to an assisted living facility for rehabilitation. Altogether, she spent nearly three months between the hospital and rehab.

What did she do during all that time? She made friends with everyone. Doctors, nurses, therapists—by the time she left, they all knew her. They loved her cheerful attitude and her constant encouragement.

I stayed with her every day and every night. At the hospital I slept on a small cot. At the rehabilitation facility I slept in a folding chair.

Rick was incredible through it all. The hospital fed Fonda, but I still needed meals. Rick brought food every day and usually included a few sweet treats for Fonda. In the evenings he would take me home so I could shower and then drive me back so I could spend the night with her again.

When Fonda finally left the rehabilitation center, many of the staff members told her they were sorry to see her go. Of course they were happy she was recovering, but they had grown fond of her kindness and her bright smile.

Sometimes it seems that here in Utah, if Fonda isn't in the hospital, I am. Thankfully, most of the time we both feel well and remain positive, although all those doctor visits can certainly be inconvenient.

I continued seeing Dr. Chidester every three months. On May 1, 2025, he informed me that the bladder cancer had returned once again. I had my fourth surgery on May 6. This time he also used a small amount of chemotherapy, which thankfully caused no noticeable side effects. As always, Fonda and Rick were with me the entire time.

Because the cancer kept returning, Dr. Chidester referred me to another specialist, Dr. David Gill. Dr. Gill recommended a newer treatment involving targeted infusions—similar to chemotherapy but designed to affect only a small area of the body. The name of the treatment was Adstiladrin. I couldn't even pronounce the name and had no idea what the treatment was. But if the doctors recommended it, I would take it.

The schedule became routine: lab work on Monday, a doctor's visit on Tuesday, and the infusion treatment on Wednesday. I received these treatments once every three months for a year. My final treatment occurred on March 18, 2026, shortly before this book was published. So far, the bladder cancer has not returned.

Looking back, I realize how fortunate we have been. We have been blessed with skilled doctors, compassionate nurses, and the constant support of family. And through it all, Fonda and I continue to look forward to many more years together, filled with love, life and laughter.

CHAPTER FOURTEEN

Seven Keys to a Happy Marriage

Profound Patience and Mutual Support

A major key to our long marriage is the profound patience and selfless support we've shared for one another's endeavors. When I was involved in basic military training, Fonda woke up early to mend my uniforms, cook my meals, and even "spit shine" my boots. Later, when I was completing my master's thesis, she stayed up from midnight to 6:00 a.m. typing more than 3,000 pages for me on a manual typewriter. At the graduation services, Georgia Tech awarded wives of graduates a degree: an MPHE, or "Mistress of Patience in Husband Engineering". The college president and I signed the graduation certificate.

Prioritizing Regular Date Nights

Even when we were heavily in debt and I was working 50 to 60 hours a week, we made sure to go on a date every Friday night. We often went to a local restaurant, Logan's Roadhouse. Fonda was so kind to the server, that on her last day at the restaurant, the server actually gave us a tip instead of accepting a tip from us. What a surprise.

Shared Faith and Serving Others

A deep, shared commitment to our faith and to helping others has always united us. After studying for eight years, we were baptized into The Church of Jesus Christ of Latter-day Saints and later traveled to the Salt Lake Temple to be sealed together for "time and all eternity." We also served a three-year church mission together in Idaho. Furthermore, Fonda often called me "disaster man" because we consistently volunteered side-by-side during major natural disasters, working tirelessly to clear debris and help victims of Hurricane Andrew, Hurricane Katrina, and multiple devastating floods and tornadoes.

Keeping Humor and Playfulness Alive

Our relationship has always been full of laughter, teasing, and not taking life too seriously. As high school sweethearts, I once tricked Fonda into eating rattlesnake at a dinner party. Years later, our family tricked a terrified Fonda into riding *Space Mountain* at Disney World, resulting in her jokingly threatening to banish us all to "outer darkness". I also once slipped a pager into her purse before she started playing the organ during a quiet church service, creating an embarrassing moment for us both when the pager unexpectedly went off. We later laughed about it.

Facing Hardships and Health Crises as a Team

When Fonda was diagnosed with multiple sclerosis, I refused to give up and began searching for treatments. We both committed to a highly restrictive, low-fat diet designed by Dr. Roy Swank, which allowed Fonda to live virtually symptom-free for over thirty-five years. I must admit, I was not that good at staying on the diet, but Fonda followed it diligently. We have also constantly stayed by each other's side in the hospital through multiple broken hips and my aggressive bladder cancer treatments. We were together at the devastating loss of our daughter, Mitzi, to breast cancer.

Constant Affection and Expressing Appreciation

I never stopped trying to impress Fonda and express my love for her. In high school, I wrote her romantic poems and sonnets, trying to find words to describe her beauty and character. I constantly acknowledge her sweet nature and how she cares for me; I still remember how, whenever I was tired and grumpy from working, Fonda would simply give me a big kiss and tell me how much she loved me—which I admit sometimes made me want to act grumpy just to get the kiss.

Embracing Adventure and Making Memories

Throughout our lives, we have always shared adventures together. When we had very little money, we camped in a small tent to attend the New York and Montreal World's Fairs. In our mid-sixties, we joined a rugged wilderness therapy program in the Arizona desert, surviving freezing rain and trying to learn to start fires without matches. To celebrate our 50th wedding anniversary, we traveled from Florida all the way to Alaska, where we rode a UTV through the wilderness and watched glaciers slide into the sea. Fonda and I have visited all 50 states together.

About the Author

Ritchey Marbury spent most of his life as a professional civil engineer and professional land surveyor. He started working with his father at age eleven, working during the summers.

He met the love of his life, Fonda Starnes, on a bus trip with their high school band. When she lost her purse and another boy found it, he took the purse from the boy who found it so he could take it to Fonda and meet her. They married seven years later.

After serving with the U. S. Army Corps of Engineers for two years, he returned to work with his father, later serving as president of Marbury Engineering Company. After he turned 65, he sold his company but continued to work in various positions in the engineering and surveying profession, as he did not wish to retire.

He continued to work full-time until the age of 83, when he retired and moved from Albany, Georgia to Herriman, Utah. Now, at age 87, he continues to do limited engineering consulting and maintains his professional engineering license in Georgia.

The loves of his life are his wife, children, grandchildren, and great grandchildren.

www.ingramcontent.com/pod-product-compliance
Ingram Content Group UK Ltd.
Pitfield, Milton Keynes, MK11 3LW, UK
UKHW021909190726
13853UKWH00002B/578